# Tensions Between Capitalism and Democracy Today From the Perspective of J. S. Mill and J. A. Schumpeter

Gülenay Baş Dinar • Çınla Akdere

# Tensions Between Capitalism and Democracy Today From the Perspective of J. S. Mill and J. A. Schumpeter

palgrave
macmillan

Gülenay Baş Dinar
Department of Economics
Bolu Abant Izzet Baysal University
Bolu, Türkiye

Çınla Akdere
Department of Economics
Middle East Technical University
Ankara, Türkiye

ISBN 978-3-031-45546-9 ISBN 978-3-031-45547-6 (eBook)
https://doi.org/10.1007/978-3-031-45547-6



This Palgrave Macmillan imprint is published by the registered company Springer Nature Switzerland AG.
The registered company address is: Gewerbestrasse 11, 6330 Cham, Switzerland

Paper in this product is recyclable.

# Preface

The book is an attempt to show how the economic and political theories of J. S. Mill (1806–1873) and J. A. Schumpeter (1883–1950) may help us to understand the present structure of capitalism over the relationship with democracy. The dominant factors in the functioning of today's capitalism, such as authoritarianism of states under the pressure of elite power, the erosion of democracy, and the dominance of different elites will be discussed in light of the economic and political analyses of Mill and Schumpeter.

The role of elites in today's capitalism is explained either through purely economic categories such as public choice theory or through purely political categories such as democratic elite theories. Purely political or purely economic explanations of elites are insufficient, as they deal with the issue and do not consider the interaction between these two areas. Both of these explanations fall short of understanding the growing role of elites in the functioning of contemporary capitalism. Mill and Schumpeter's analyses offer a superior analysis compared to these approaches since they combine economic and political aspects.

Both theories help us to understand the economic power and the economic role of elites in the functioning of a capitalist economy and liberal political system. Hence, they have contributed to political science focusing on the role of commercial and governmental elites in the functioning of the capitalist system. No book has ever discussed them together, emphasizing the common and different points of their theories revealing today's world where states have increasingly greater economic and political influence.

The reason why we focus especially on Mill and Schumpeter is their liberal approaches deal with economic and political analysis together in a holistic context and build all their analyses on this integrity. In addition, both thinkers offered theoretical explanations about the basic and variable economic and political structure of capitalism while having been interested in socialism. On one hand, Mill interrogates the practical organization of the government. On the other hand, through the concept of creative destruction, Schumpeter argues that the capitalist system will gradually become a corporatist structure, and it will reconcile with the state and society in a socialist order to maintain profitability after a certain period of time. Both economists attached great importance to the coexistence of economic and political processes to present a realistic analysis of capitalism.

Bolu and Ankara, Turkey
June 2023

Gülenay Baş Dinar
Çınla Akdere

# Contents

# About the Authors

**Gülenay Baş Dinar** is Professor at Abant İzzet Baysal University, Department of Economics. She completed her undergraduate and graduate education at Abant İzzet Baysal University in the Department of Economics, and obtained her doctorate degree at the Hacettepe University Social Sciences Institute, Department of Economics. Her thesis at Utah University, USA is based on six months of research through the doctoral research scholarship of the Higher Education Institution of Turkey. She has written articles and book chapters on the history of economic thought.

**Çınla Akdere** is Assistant Professor at Middle East Technical University, Department of Economics. She received her bachelor's degree from Ankara University, Faculty of Political Sciences, Department of Economics, and her master's and doctorate degrees in the history of economic thought from Université Paris I Panthéon-Sorbonne. She was a visiting researcher at the New School for Social Research Department of Economics for one year. She taught economics at Université Paris I Panthéon-Sorbonne, Université Cergy-Pontoise, and Université Paris VIII Vincennes Saint-Denis. She has published in national and international academic journals. She is the author of *L'Arrière-plan philosophique de l'économie politique de John Stuart Mill* by Classiques Garnier. She has been a researcher affiliated with the research institute PHARE (Philosophie, Histoire et Analyse des Représentations Économiques) since 2003 and a faculty member at the Department of Economics at Middle East Technical University (METU) since 2010. She also studied in the General and Comparative Literature Department of Université Sorbonne Nouvelle-Paris III.

CHAPTER 1

# Introduction: Why We Read Mill and Schumpeter Today?

**Abstract** Historically, democracy has been considered identical to liberalism as a political regime, and the concept of liberal democracy has been used to describe this approach. Thus, there has been a correlation between the development of democracy and liberalism. The development of capitalism during the nineteenth century led to a conflict between the economic inequality induced by capitalism and equality, freedom, and justice demand of the masses. J. S. Mill (1806–1873) and J. A. Schumpeter (1883–1950) were aware of the conflict between freedom and equality in liberal democratic theory. It was hardly noticed that Mill's ideas would enlighten our approach to the current conflict between capitalism and democracy. It was argued that the studies on Mill mainly helped us understand his era. Schumpeter was another philosopher who identified the conflict between democracy and capitalism and attempted to come up with a solution. Schumpeter prioritized the representative democracy and political participation approach developed by Mill in the nineteenth century and his ideas about the role of elites in democracy.

**Keywords** Democracy • Capitalism • Methodological individualism • J. S. Mill • J. A. Schumpeter


G. Baş Dinar, Ç. Akdere, *Tensions Between Capitalism and Democracy Today From the Perspective of J. S. Mill and J. A. Schumpeter*, https://doi.org/10.1007/978-3-031-45547-6_1

Why is the tension between capitalism and democracy? As put by Iversen and Soskice (2019, 17), democracy and capitalism have a symbiotic relationship. Democracy and capitalism are considered semiotically associated political and economic systems. Since M. Friedman's (1912–2006) famous book *Capitalism and Freedom* ([1962]2002), the idea of the duality of liberal democracy and capitalism has become predominant. Thus, economic freedom was considered a prerequisite of political freedom, and subsequent studies attempted to demonstrate this approach (Haan and Sturm 2003; Rode and Gwartney 2012 cited by Bilir and Şahin 2021). Furthermore, industrialization and democratization have been historically associated with advanced democracy, and these were called capitalist democracies. This approach was normal in Friedman's time because democratic regimes became synonymous with capitalism and authoritarian regimes with closed economic systems during the Cold War era. The correlation between democracy and capitalism should be questioned. As stated by Bilir and Şahin (2021), "neither the democratic doctrine has been suddenly established in societies, nor has capitalism always been the guarantee of individual freedoms" (Bilir and Şahin 2021, 265).

The link between capitalism and democracy is sometimes established by the distribution of income and sometimes by income level. Rueschemeyer et al. (1992 cited by Iversen and Soskice 2019, 136) emphasized this link by emphasizing the power induced by low income, not by high income, focusing on a different facet of industrialization. This facet opposed the power of the masses and elites, arguing that, "industrialization leads to working-class power" and "often with left-liberal and sometimes left catholic support, pressuring the elites to concede political representation" (Iversen and Soskice 2019, 136).

The book clearly put forward the link between the history of economic thought and contemporary economic and political theories. We adopt a heuristic method called the "intensive approach" by A. Lapidus (1996). This approach corresponds to the symbiotic nature of economic theory and the history of economic thought: "it does not deal with either the past or the established present, but with the transformation of the present of the discipline" (Lapidus 1996, 867). Whereas other heuristic methods, mentioning especially "retrospective approach" (interpreting a set of old statements according to the problems in force at the time when they have been established) and "extensive approach" (constrained by the present state of economic knowledge, is doomed to letting filter from an ancient knowledge that what she is able to interpret in contemporary terms). The retrospective approach "allows the identification of modem issues of old problematics" (Lapidus 1996, 867). "Intensive approach" presents not only the state of economic knowledge but also its transformation through the reactivation of ancient knowledge (Lapidus 1996, 867, 2019).

Historically, democracy has been considered identical to liberalism as a political regime, and the concept of liberal democracy has been used to describe this approach. Thus, there has been a correlation between the development of democracy and liberalism. Liberal theory was developed in the seventeenth century as the ideology of the capitalist system and analyzed what is good and what is bad for people and society (Şaylan 1998, 27). In capitalism, democracy became the mainstay of the struggle of the bourgeoisie with aristocracy. Liberalism advocated the contract, equality before the law, and sovereignty of the people, namely, the foundations of democracy, against the rigid and hierarchical structure of feudal society. Due to these values, it could be suggested that the liberal approach initially was a progressive ideology. Its progressive foundation led to broad acceptance of liberalism, and it proliferated during the nineteenth and twentieth centuries. Liberalism advocated values such as equality, justice, and freedom for all, not for a specific elite class or group. The values that liberalism advocated for the masses started to pose a threat to capitalism over time.

The development of capitalism during the nineteenth century led to a conflict between the economic inequality induced by capitalism and equality, freedom, and justice demand of the masses. The opposition of the working masses increased against the capitalist system in the second half of the nineteenth century. Due to the threat of the working class to overthrow capitalism, the bourgeoisie had to consolidate its position as a class. This led to the redefinition of the ideals of democracy, such as equality, freedom, and justice, to preserve the authority of the capitalists. These principles, on which the new liberal approach to democracy was based, can be observed in the works of liberal philosophers such as John Locke (1623–1704) and J. S. Mill (1806–1873). These philosophers reconsidered democratic ideals, equality, and freedom to prevent the abolition of private property (Lichtman 2012, 218, 219). They basically reduced equality to a formal equality before the law and freedom to equal participation in public life.

Mill lived in a period of significant social change led by the industrial revolution. This period, under the significant impact of liberal discourse, witnessed serious social tension and conflict. Mill was deeply committed to the liberal tradition with an emphasis on freedom and aware that the social injustice induced by capitalism would seriously damage freedoms. According to Mill, freedom was the most important value that should be protected. In *On Liberty* ([1859]1977b), he argued that human freedom was threatened by two factors: the threat from above and the threat from below. The reduction of freedom of expression posed the threat from above, while the demands of the masses that he described as the tyranny of the majority posed the threat from below. Mill claimed that freedoms could be restricted when these threats are serious. According to Mill, the tyranny of the majority could be in the form of a political majority that would attempt to redistribute wealth and property. He indicated that this would interfere with the right to property and freedom and suggested that voting rights could be limited to those who would not attempt to redistribute property rights to prevent such a threat (Şaylan 1998, 42, 43).

This Millian idea was the basis of the liberal idea that although authority is determined by the majority, the former could not interfere with the natural rights and freedoms of the individual. Since individual rights and freedoms were largely defined by the right of property, this led to a conflict between freedom and equality. Thus, the efforts to ensure equality harmed the right to property, which liberals considered a basic individual right and freedom. Adversely, unrestricted right to property would also damage equality among the individuals, underlying the conflict between capitalism and democracy. Capitalism is a system of individual freedoms. In the capitalist system, one of the most fundamental individual freedoms is the freedom to acquire property and accumulate wealth. However, the right to property and wealth led to economic inequality, undermining the democratic ideal of equality.

Although the relationship between capitalism and democracy has been controversial since the beginning, after World War II, there was a period when the relationship between liberal capitalism and democracy was quite strong. After World War II, the world witnessed a series of historical conditions that led to an expansion period with rapid and relatively stable capital accumulation. The rapid economic growth in this period, called democratic capitalism or the Keynesian welfare state, increased the power of the working class and allowed the implementation of their democratic demands. This period of rapid capital accumulation, high profitability and high demand for labor reconciled the interests of the capitalist and working classes.

However, the crisis of the early 1970s destroyed the compromise between the working and capitalist classes. Then, the neoliberal policies adopted to end the crisis and restore profitability revealed the incompatibility of liberal democracy with capitalism. Neoliberalism, which meant the redistribution of wealth in favor of the capitalist class, gradually became anti-democratic since neoliberal public policies and reorganization of the distribution of wealth were only possible through government sanctions. The gains of the working class during the period of a relatively strong relationship between democracy and capitalism were lost due to constitutional changes. Dardot and Laval (2019) argued that a new neoliberal authority was established through the enactment of economic and law enforcement measures of war. To prevent and solve the social, economic and political crises of this period, governments had to adopt a set of rules that eliminated and limited the resistance of the workers by excluding the collective (Dardot and Laval 2019, 31).

Furthermore, globalization complemented neoliberal policies that allowed developed capitalist nations to end the crisis. International institutions such as the World Bank, the International Monetary Fund, and the World Trade Organization became intermediaries in the globalization of neoliberal policies. These neoliberal policies imposed by the abovementioned institutions on developing countries seriously weakened nation states. During globalization, nation states remained unresponsive to the social demands of their citizens since they were forced to implement the neoliberal policies imposed by these institutions. They even suppressed these demands with anti-democratic policies. The fall of the Berlin Wall in 1989 and the disintegration of the Soviet Union popularized the idea that socialism was no longer an option and that the liberal capitalist system had no alternative. Fukuyama's "*End of History*" (1989) thesis declared the ideological victory of neoliberalism. The ideological prevalence of neoliberalism during the 1990s and early 2000s led to the erosion of democracy and political participation in nation states.

Neoliberal policies led to a significant reduction in the economic power of the working class. Neoliberal policies allowed the determination of wages by the market, weakened social rights, and introduced certain incentives and conveniences for capitalists. In this period, the damage caused by neoliberal policies in working class income was tried to be eliminated by financialization. Financialization allowed the working class, whose purchasing power has decreased due to neoliberal policies and who increasingly impoverished, to borrow cheap loans in financial markets to maintain consumption. On the one hand, financialization helped overcome the recession by ensuring continuous demand; on the other hand, it prevented the working class revolution by pacifying them via loans. Indebted workers were more hesitant to defend their democratic rights when the system was weak.

The financialization strategy adopted during the 1990s paved the way for the crisis of 2008. This crisis deepened the conflict between democracy and liberalism and paved the way for further anti-democratic practices. The policies adopted after the crisis of 2008 aimed to compensate for the losses of the large financial corporations that were responsible for the crisis. The "occupy Wall Street" was a response to government policies that prioritized the interests of the top1%.

T. Piketty's book *Capital in the Twenty-First Century*, published in 2014, emphasized that the most important problem of contemporary capitalism was inequality. The problem of inequality was an issue that liberal democracy trivialized. Today, however, the consequences of inequality threaten the future of both capitalism and democracy. Thus, the liberal capitalist approach that reduced democracy to market freedom could no longer convince the masses. Currently, more egalitarian projects that aim to redistribute the wealth of the upper income groups to the lower income groups have become extremely important for the survival of capitalism.

The evolution of capitalist society reached a stage that could be described as "the postpandemic stage". This argument is necessary since the postpandemic era has its own characteristics. First, it should be characterized by high inflation, called "post-COVID inflation", induced by extreme monetary supply during the pandemic (Harding, Lindé and Trabandt 2023). Current capitalism could be characterized by inflation, the problems of the consumer who struggled with inflation, and the self-propagating capital growth that never existed in history. The first character is more seasonal, while the latter is systemic. Contemporary inflation could be explained by a combination of demand and supply shock observed during the pandemic, beyond the natural function of the system. It has been questioned whether the inflation was transient (Nationwide Economics 2023). Cascaldi-Garcia, Orak and Saijid (2023) argued that inflation was predominantly experienced in food, energy, and commodity industries worldwide. Bernstein and Tedeschi (2021) described the inflation induced by the pandemic as an "unconventional recession". Harding, Lindé and Trabandt (2023) employed the Phillips curve to explain inflation and asked the following question: "Has the Phillips curve steepened or are large exogenous demand and supply factors key to understanding why inflation has risen so much?" They attempted to answer this question with the macroeconomic model constructed with the nonlinear Phillips curve that included all shocks.

The most important effect of postpandemic inflation has been the increase in economic inequality. The pandemic exacerbated the negative consequences of the neoliberal economy, especially in the health and education sectors. Liberal capitalist ideology considered inequality a natural outcome of just, fair and rational development. According to liberal theory, intelligence, skills, etc., of the individuals is not equal; thus, smarter and more resourceful individuals would be rewarded more due to the market conditions. Therefore, economic inequalities due to market relations were considered just and fair in liberal theory. This was also one of the reasons why liberals opposed interventions in the market economy. Market interventions would prevent rewarding smarter, more skilled and talented individuals. What liberal theorists meant by equality was equality before the law and equality in fundamental rights and freedoms (Şaylan 1998, 56).

Mill was aware of the conflict between freedom and equality in liberal democratic theory. This was largely due to the interest of Mill in both liberal and socialist philosophies. This led to significant differences between his written ideas. He praised laissez-faire in *On Liberty* ([1859]1977b), while he critiqued liberal culture in *The Principles of Political Economy* ([1848]1965). When Mill promoted freedom and democracy, he was aware of the inhumane consequences of capitalism, which led Mill to adopt a more critical attitude toward capitalism later in his life. A nineteenth century philosopher, Mill's initial mission was to promote the right to property against the threat of the abolishment of private property by the political majority that he called the tyranny of the majority, then he approached socialist ideology when he emphasized the negative consequences of inequality due to capitalism. In *Considerations on Representative Government Mill* ([1861]1977a), the Millian political question focused on the self-actualization of individuals. Thus, the primary function of the government should be to promote the virtue and intelligence of the individuals who are the foundation of society. According to Mill, the government played an instrumental role in individual achievements (Lichtman 2012, 236, 237).

It was hardly noticed that Mill's ideas would enlighten our approach to the current conflict between capitalism and democracy. It was argued that the studies on Mill mainly helped us understand his era. Then, one day someone asked the following question: "Why read Mill today?" This question was the title of the book by the moral philosopher J. Skorupski, and he was fortunate to have selected this title. He demonstrated that the Millian approach should not be forgotten in the dusty shelves of history. He emphasized that we could learn a lot about today from his social and political ideas. He listed the approaches associated with democracy and governance in a few questions: "What Mill feared about democracy was majoritarian despotism and conformist mediocrity. What he hoped was that it would be the greatest school of self-governance. He was both a moral and cultural elitist and an optimistic political and civic egalitarian" (Skorupski 2006, 96). These questions were experienced in the political and economic governance of several countries. Skorupski argued that the content of Mill's narrative was suitable democratic philosophy, and he emphasized two significant fears. The first was extreme pessimism about the decline of democracy "to mediocrity", and the second was optimism about the "virtue of self-governance" (Skorupski 2006, 97).

J. A. Schumpeter (1883–1950) was another philosopher who identified the conflict between democracy and capitalism and attempted to come up with a solution. Schumpeter's era witnessed the escalation of the conflict between capitalism and democracy. In this period, the 1929 Depression and rising fascism in Europe led to a debate on the relationship between democracy and capitalism and the future of capitalism and democracy. In *Capitalism, Socialism and Democracy*[1] ([1942]2008), Schumpeter initiated the discussion on the sustainability of capitalism. Schumpeter's response was negative. He, similar to K. Marx (1818–1883), emphasized that capitalism was internally unstable and prone to collapse. However, unlike Marx, Schumpeterian reason was not the failure of the system but its success. In the capitalist system, entrepreneurs and innovations, namely, the driving force of the system, lead to creative destruction. This driving force of the system would constantly destroy the old system and replace it with a new one, leading to an environment of constant change and revolution. Thus, the evolution of capitalism into a monopolistic phase due to competition would routinize entrepreneurship and innovation, and capitalism would lose its dynamics from within. Schumpeter emphasized that the decline in capitalism would lead to a weak democracy. He argued that capitalism was more democratic than socialism. He claimed that the

[1] Hereafter *CSD*.

current democracy was a representative democracy, where citizens only elect the rulers that would prioritize their concerns. This Schumpeterian analysis in *CSD* was a quite accurate analysis of the parliamentary systems of today.

This is a detail that Schumpeter commentators often neglect. For some reason, Schumpeter's arguments about the future of capitalism have always been analyzed based only on economics. Specifically, Özveren (2000) argued that Schumpeter applied the concept of "economic competition" to the political realm: the quest of political parties for representation of the populace as one of competition." For him, as the economy as a dynamic capitalist process was motivated by an entrepreneurial quest for profit and a strong sense of rivalry in the sense of classical competition, the study of the political domain with a focus on democracy. However, in this displacement, politicians also needed to innovate: "leaders were to the political function what his entrepreneurs were to all important entrepreneurial functions. Just as the entrepreneurs introduced new combinations, or applied economical inventions that could have been neglected for quite some time, political leaders articulated and shaped groupwise volitions" (Özveren 2000, 52). However, political events also lead to the conditions that prepare "creative destruction", self-destruction of capitalism, and the transition to socialism. As there is mutual causality between these two processes, "technocratic authoritarianism" would dominate the future, which is "a product of capitalist technological evolution, coupled with an unlimited individualism whereby the individual may become virtually paralyzed" (Özveren 2000, 64).

Consistent with that approach, Schumpeter discussed the operation of the democratic system and the role of elites based on competition and emphasized that majority rule was impossible in practice. On the one hand, Schumpeter stressed that the "rule of the majority" suggested by the conventional approach to democracy was impossible, and on the other hand, he argued that representative democracy was the best possible form of democracy. Thus, the ruling elite was not considered an obstacle to democracy in Schumpeter's analysis. In contrast, elites were considered necessary for active democracy. Schumpeter's ideas were almost a response to Mill, who discussed the same topic a century before him. In Mill's analysis of the freedoms that led to the development of the capitalist system, he also discussed the democratic system. Thus, Mill also considered representative democracy to be the best form of democracy. Due to the economic, social and political realities of their time, the central issue for

Schumpeter and Mill was the function of the elites in democracy. Schumpeter considered democracy a competition between the elites, and Mill stressed their significance in ruling classes.

Schumpeter was a good Mill reader. In the *History of Economic Analysis* (1954), he cited Mill on several issues, including his utilitarian approach to economic methodology, the accumulation of capital, and his view on the stationary state. If Schumpeter's primary fetish economist was Marx, Mill was the second. Schumpeter covered almost all economic topics that Mill discussed. He emphasized the differences between Mill and Smith and between Malthus and Ricardo. These underlined the significance of institutions in Millian economics. For example, "custom". However, this book was not written to interpret Schumpeter's views on Mill. It was written to discuss their similarities and differences when addressing various issues. The main objective was to emphasize the conflict between capitalism and democracy that has existed since time immemorial, which is a "blind spot" in both economics and political science.

Certain disciplines have analyzed the conflict between capitalism and democracy based on rent, incentivization of regulations, etc. Two of these, namely, political science and sociology, associated the conflict with social classes. Mainstream and neoclassical economics were never interested in the conflict between capitalism and democracy. Thus, this conflict has been in the "blind spot" of these three disciplines. Thus, related studies have been rare (Holcombe 2016). The current book aims to see the "blind spot" that both economics and political science could not see due to the lack of a methodology and to determine related mechanisms. Thus, instead of discussing the researchers in these three disciplines, the book focuses on the work of two economists, namely, Mill and Schumpeter, who analyzed the conflict between capitalism and democracy from a significant and well-equipped perspective based on the history of economic philosophy. The book attempts to demonstrate how Millian and Schumpeterian doctrines could help understand today.

The history of economic philosophy is full of economists who explained different stages of the capitalist system based on economic and social functions. However, only a few discussed the political conditions that led to capitalist accumulation. Mill and Schumpeter could help understand the duality of democracy and capitalism, since they introduced a general economic doctrine that approached both economic and political dimensions. They were the two important philosophers who noticed the conflict between democracy and capitalism at an early stage. Both are associated with the crises of democracy and capitalism. Both Mill and Schumpeter criticized the classical liberal democracy based on public participation and agreed that only possible democracy was representative democracy. They defended their analysis of the elites based on this fact. If the direct democracy advocated by liberals was not possible and the only possible democracy was representative democracy, then how could democracy function better under these conditions? Thus, both pondered the question of how democracy was possible and how it could be improved rather than defending the ideal of democracy.

The current conflict in capitalism indicates the power of giant corporations that were empowered by high capital accumulation over the state. Bilir and Şahin (2021) argued that this threatens the economic system. However, it is also a major threat to politics. This threat is manifested in two ways. First, the economic power of giant corporations affects government policies, and second, bosses rule the country like a business. Both have actually happened. An example for the first case was the pressure applied by Marc Zuckerberg on the state to acquire the power to print money by introducing a currency (Libra) valid only in Facebook. An example of the second is the election of Donald Trump. The book aims to discuss these dominant factors that affected the complex operation of current capitalism and the democratic transformation induced by these factors. If a capitalist crisis is in fact experienced, it could be understood not by a discussion of theoretical dynamics but by the political background that reinforced it in a certain way.

Political scientists have discussed two aspects of democracy: substantive and formal. Formal elements of democracy have developed in liberal democratic capitalism, where democracy and capitalism were considered synonymous, and democracy had an institutional framework called representative democracy. Today, it could be argued that representative democracy that prioritizes the formal elements of democracy is also in crisis. It could be suggested that representative democracy has been in crisis since the beginning of the neoliberal era. Today, democracy and political participation are reduced to the electoral process, and participation in political life ceased to be a primary goal in representing the interests and welfare of the masses that has been the essence of democracy. Furthermore, the participation of the individual in politics has decreased significantly, even in elections. However, one of the most important pillars of liberal democracy has been the participation of the individual in political life. In a representative democracy, the individual should actualize the freedom to elect and be elected. However, in modern society, the political participation of the individual decreased significantly in both elections and representation. Furthermore, hidden power relations exist behind the political decisions that concern most of society. These powers that entail direct economic, political and economic processes affect important government decisions that the entire society, seriously contradicting essential democratic values.

R. G. Holcombe (2016) and B. Milanovic (2019) called the collaboration of elites "political capitalism", where both political and economic interests affect each other. This concept, which described the balance of power in the current capitalist system quite well, meant that the elites guided the state based on their interests. They do this via legislation, government spending, and the tax system. The incentives they provide to others return to political elites with the support of the economic elites, and the former could maintain their status. The process is a dual process of continuity and unlimited renewal of mutual interests that benefit both political and economic elites. Private rent, bribery to pass the desired laws, extortion, interest group contributions to political campaigns, and employment of family members in various public posts are concrete examples of this dual relation of interest. The political participation of the masses and their presence are supported as long as they do not challenge the elites (Holcombe 2016, 115–120).

Holcombe (2016, 105) sought answers to the question about the duty of the state. Is it simply to protect people's well-being or the economic well-being as well? The regulation of economic power was considered one of the duties of the state. However, regulation was also controlled and manipulated by economic power. Political capitalism analyzes the correlations between politics and economy and focuses on the relations between the elites and the state. In that sense, it goes beyond the public choice theory because it tackles the economic roles of the state, the elected government, and the electorate. It considered all stakeholders as individuals and their decisions as individual decisions that protected their interests. The social approach of these two theories was dualistic (Holcombe 2016). E. F. Toma (2014, 895) argued that, "public choice modified the traditional model to allow not only market failure but also government failure."

This dualism can be expressed in different terms: elites and masses, or 1% and 99%. Public choice theory, after the contributions of Olson (1965) and Stigler (1971), became closer to neoclassical economic theories and distanced itself from classical political economy since it considered developing social classes as "interest groups". The "disproportionate representation" of corporations, collaborations, and professional groups in politics was close to "majoritarian pluralism". This doctrine, which argued that the state's favoritism was the most important characteristic of capitalism, could be discussed based on the public bailout of corporations, subsidies granted to companies with political connections, and the FED assistance to certain banks during the crisis of 2008. This was also coined "crony capitalism" (Holcombe 2016). Hence, the most important feature of recent capitalism has become the control of business (here "business" referred to main economic interests) over politics rather than the political regulation of the economy. This manipulation reached such levels that it "designed and controlled political institutions for their advantage" (Holcombe 2016, 105).

Democracy essentially aims for the sovereignty of the people but not that of certain privileged elites. The existence of the abovementioned centers of influence called lobbies that could manipulate the government indicates that current democracies cannot ensure political equality. Furthermore, one of the main pillars of classical democracy theory was the assumption that people are rational. Thus, for democracy to work, individuals should know their needs and expectations from the government. It was assumed that rational individuals would choose the best among the available alternatives. However, for the independent will of the people, the individual should know her or his needs and could select the most beneficial one among the political options. On the one hand, this depends on the advanced analysis skills of the individual, and on the other hand, availability of the required information. Currently, however, individuals are only informed by the media. However, an individual's access to information is quite limited since information is considered a commodity produced and distributed in the market in developed capitalist societies. Furthermore, the aim of oligopolistic media is only advertising profits rather than providing accurate political information. Today, election campaigns are organized by professional advertising and public relations specialists. The images and themes that determine voter preferences are prioritized, and the content and coherence of the public policy proposals are not discussed effectively. The organization of election campaigns by such professionals increases the cost of election campaigns, and financing these campaigns has become rather difficult. Concessions made to finance elections could lead to significant problems in democratic values and practices (Şaylan 1998, 74–78).

## Methodological Individualism and Some of Its Ambivalences

Public choice theory, also called social choice theory, investigates the role of the state in the political behavior of voters, elected officials, civil servants, and interest groups. In other words, it questions the rational behavior of individuals and social groups. Similar to neoclassical theories, it was founded on "methodological individualism", where the baseline was the individual. Thus, it is assumed that the individual always makes rational decisions. It transferred these methods and assumptions to the realm of political science. According to this theory, political decisions are the sum of individual decisions based only on self-interest. Politicians and civil servants were considered consumers or producers of economic theory; however, the institutional structure was different, and they usually did not spend their own money, thus leading to the Millian (J. S. Mill) context. In modern literature, the "principal-agent problem" could be observed when representatives do not act based on the interests of their constituencies (or act for self-interest) (Holcombe 2016).

The methodological approaches of Mill and Schumpeter were quite similar. The primary aim of both Mill and Schumpeter was to explain the function of the capitalist system beginning with the individual. The term "methodological individualism" was christened by Schumpeter in *Das Wesen und der Hauptinhalt der theoretischen* Nationalökonomie published in 1908. The article "On the concept of social value" published in the *Quarterly Journal of Economics* a year after *Das Wesen und der Hauptinhalt der theoretischen Nationalökonomie* was the first known use of the term in English literature (Schumpeter 1909, 231). Schumpeter's (1909) goal was to establish a philosophical basis for his analysis of economic demand: "individuals demand certain goods: the only important point is that all things are demanded, produced, and paid for because individuals want them" (Schumpeter 1909, 216).

Mill described in his works on liberalism a world where politicians were motivated to maximize self-interest—including the collective interest according to Mill—and to ensure re-election. Mill individualized the representatives and attributed to them the characteristics he reserved for *homo economicus*. Mill considered political economy an independent and unique field of social sciences. He argued that social phenomena were "complex" and an outcome of only an "intermixture of causes". These, he claimed, included psychological, cultural or economic factors. This science argued that individuals were motivated by the "desire of wealth", and the two most important brakes against this desire were "aversion to labor" and the "desire to enjoy costly indulgences" (Mill [1836]2003, 322; Mill [1843]1973, 902). This deep desire demonstrated that an individual would always prefer more to less. Similar to the *homo economicus*, the representative government could give up current interests to achieve its true objectives: "Mill considered the 'guidance of [the laboring poor's] conduct by their real ultimate interest, as opposed to their immediate and apparent interest' as one of the guiding principles of a civilized representative state" (Tyler 2006, 347; Mill [1861]1977a, 107).

G. Hodgson emphasized the influence of Max Weber (1968), Schumpeter's teacher, who "promoted a position that has since been described as methodological individualism in the first chapter of his *Economy and Society*, published after his death in 1920" (Hodgson 2007, 212). However, the idea dates back to Mill's work. Mill could be considered the frontrunner of methodological individualism before Schumpeter christened the concept. This method shaped his economic, moral and political theories. According to Mill's methodological individualism and as a part of his economic epistemology, economic theory is centered on an individual's incentives and interests. In Book VI of *System of Logic*, Mill asked the following: "To judge how he will act under the variety of desires and aversions which are concurrently operating upon him, we must know how he would act under the exclusive influence of each one in particular." (Mill [1836]2003, 322) He identified three incentives for the individual: The first was the general incentive, the desire for wealth, the second was aversion to labor, and the third was the desire for immediate joy of expensive pleasures (Mill [1836]2003, 322; Mill [1843]1973, 902). The second and third incentives were considered obstacles to the desire for wealth.

Mill aimed to describe, explain or even measure individual acts under the influence of each of these factors. Mill was aware of the absurdity of that abstract human as the subject matter of social acts. He called it the "geometrical individual" and emphasized that, that individual acts within society. Mill's "geometrical individual" remained a description of economic rationality for a long time. As new economic theories with new descriptions of economic rationality were proposed, Mill's approach provided a background.

Nevertheless, a description of Mill's methodological individualism based only on the abovementioned economic rationality would be unfortunate; when the moral and political framework of Mill's oeuvres are considered, intertwining personal and collective interests would be obvious. On Mill's liberalism, only one idea could be proposed: the paradox between economic rationality and political rationality. Such an approach would help cover the two main dimensions of his liberal approach: economic and political dimensions. The starting point of the current discussion will also show the limits ofboth Mill and Schumpeter's methodological individualist approach. Hence, J. Agassi's "institutional individualism" (1960, 1975), which "combines individual actions and their interaction with the social context" (Zouboulakis 2002, 2–3), is associated with both authors' methods. Schumpeter's methodological individualism intersected with political individualism. We will describe the analogy between commercial and leadership competition where the government acts like an entrepreneur.

The fact that the rulers are individuals who pursue their interests is a typical methodological individualism. The definition of methodological individualism emphasizes the social nature of economic rationality (Zouboulakis 2005; Hodgson 2007). As stated by Zouboulakis (2005), the complex nature of the concept was also indicated by John Stuart Mill, who applied it to the political realm as well. In other words, the behavior of both politicians and elites should be considered in the social analysis of economic rationality.

This approach owes its existence to the individual introduced by A. Smith. Smith described the individual he studied as one who created added value through economic activities within certain geographical and historical limits (Smith 1776, 477 cited by Zouboulakis 2005). The description of the individual based on geographical and historical existence also assigned social, cultural and moral traits. Mill always emphasized that economic activities were context dependent, and their social circumstances should also be described well. Smithian methodology was consistent with this approach. The Millian "inverse deductive method" (Akdere 2021; Légé 2005), which entails both induction and deduction, demonstrates the gap between theoretical abstraction and real events. This gap was because the theory neglected certain factors that played a role in this development.

The fact that the rulers pursued their interests was consistent with the rationality hypothesis. This was about the consumer who desired to achieve maximum benefit within the limits of economic conditions and restrictions (such as consumer's budget and producer's technology) and the manufacturer who desired maximum profit. These ideas, which were introduced during the transformation of the classical political economy into the neoclassical approach, were included in the essence of the theory and purified from the socioeconomic context during the era of W. S. Jevons (1835–1882) and L. Walras (1834–1910) (Zouboulakis 2005).

However, as Hodgson (2007, 211) noted, "explanations in terms of individuals alone have never, as yet, been achieved" and furthermore, "the more feasible version of explanations in terms of individuals plus relations between them amount to the introduction of social structure alongside individuals in the explanantia". In other words, economic events that involve more than one individual are social events (Hodgson 2007, 211). This approach was in contrast with the "atomistic utilitarian tradition", in other words, to the analogy that involved economic actors and atoms. What was advocated was the embedded nature of economic activities in social relations. J. Agassi (1960, 1975) was Karl Popper's (1902–1994) student. In this discussion, he coined the term "institutional individualism" and argued that "institutional structures existed and affected individual choices, while only individuals had aims and responsibilities" (Hodgson 2007, 212).

Methodological individualism explains any social phenomenon by "reconstructing the motivations of the individuals concerned by the phenomenon in question and understanding this phenomenon as the result of the sum of individual behaviours dictated by these motivations" (Boudon 1985, 644 cited by Mouchot 2003, 214). However, in spite of its agglomerative character, the starting point for the explanation of economic relations remains the individual, or, more specifically, the decisions and actions of individuals (Hodgson 2007, 213). Hodgson (1999, 33) distinguished methodological individualism and political individualism to clarify the fact that the latter involved "individualistic ideology", without elaborating further. He described methodological individualism as the "*view that social wholes should be explained solely based on individual members*" (Hodgson 1999, 61; 1988, 1993). However, once these two types of individualism are separated, "several types of interactions between the individuals should be ignored to reach a tractable analysis" (Hodgson 1999, 61). Nevertheless, according to methodological individualism, "explanation of social structures and institutions should be inherent to individuals" (Hodgson 1999, 90).

Our book is structured into five chapters, of which this introduction shows how we approach the economic and political theories of Mill and Schumpeter. The introduction is followed by Chap. 2, where we focus on a historical presentation of the role of elites and lobbies today. This includes a definition of the concept and the power relation it creates. In Chap. 3, Mill's context will be reviewed. How the bridge between democracy and capitalism will appear in Mill's explanations on Majority Power and Elite Government. Schumpeter's description of the development of the capitalist system and the way it involves the elite will be presented in Chap. 4. In the conclusion section of Chap. 5, we state how the past or the established present is seen under the lens of Mill and Schumpeter's work.

## References


Agassi, J. 1960. Methodological individualism. *British Journal of Sociology* 11 (3): 244–270.

———. 1975. Institutional individualism. *British Journal of Sociology* 26 (2): 144–155.

Akdere, Ç. 2021. *L'Arrière-plan philosophique de l'économie politique de John Stuart Mill*. Paris: Classiques Garnier.

Bernstein, J., and E. Tedeschi. 2021. Pandemic prices: Assessing inflation in the months and years ahead. *Council of Economic Advisers: Blog*. https://www.whitehouse.gov/cea/writtenmaterials/2021/04/12/pandemic-prices-assessing-inflation-in-the-months-and-years-ahead/.

Bilir, H., and M. Şahin. 2021. Politik Ekonomiye Schumpeterci Bir Bakış: Kapitalizm ve Siyasi Elitler. *Pamukkale Üniversitesi Sosyal Bilimler Enstitüsü Dergisi* 43: 263–276.

Boudon, R. 1985. L'individualisme méthodologique. *In Encyclopedia Universalis. Supplément*. 2: 644–647.

Cascaldi-Garcia, D., M. Orak, and Z. Saijid. 2023. *Drivers of post-pandemic inflation in selected advanced economies and implications for the outlook (January 2023)*, FEDS Notes No. 2023-01-13, Available at SSRN: https://ssrn.com/abstract=4438796 or https://doi.org/10.17016/2380-7172.3232.

Dardot, P., and C. Laval. 2019. *Never ending nightmare: The neoliberal assault on democracy*. London: Verso.

De Haan, J., and J.-E. Sturm. 2003. Does more democracy lead to greater economic freedom? New evidence for developing countries. *European Journal of Political Economy* 19 (3): 547–563.

Friedman, M. [1962]2002. *Capitalism and Freedom: Fortieth Anniversary Edition*. California: The University of Chicago Press.

Fukuyama, F. 1989. The end of history? *The National Interest* 16: 3–18.

Harding, M., J. Lindé, and M. Trabandt. 2023. Understanding Post-COVID inflation dynamics. *IMF Working Paper*, WP/22/10.

Hodgson, G.M. 1988. *Economics and institutions: A manifesto for a modern institutional economics.* Cambridge and Philadephia: Polity Press and University of Pennsylvania Press.

———. 1993. *Economics and evolution: Bringing life back into economics.* Cambridge, UK and Ann Arbor, MI: Polity and University of Michigan Press.

———. 1999. Evolution and institutions. In *On the evolutionary economics and the evolution of economics.* Cheltenham: Edward Elgar.

Hodgson, G. 2007. Meanings of methodological individualism. *Journal of Economic Methodology* 14 (2): 211–226.

Holcombe, R. 2016. Politik Kapitalizm. Translated by A. Yayla. *Liberal Düşünce Dergisi* 84: 103–125. https://dergipark.org.tr/en/pub/liberal/issue/48154/609216.

Iversen, T., and D. Soskice. 2019. *Democracy and prosperity: Reinventing capitalism through a turbulent century.* Princeton and Oxford: Princeton University Press.

Lapidus, A. 1996. Introduction à une 'Histoire de la Pensée Economique' qui ne verra jamais le jour. *Revue économique* 47 (4): 867–892.

———. 2019. Bringing them alive. *European Journal of the History of Economic Thought* 25 (6): 1084–1106.

Légé, P. 2005. F. Hayek critique de John Stuart Mill: une réflexion sur la notion de justice sociale. *Economies et Sociétés, Série "Oeconomia"* 37 (10): 1819–1848.

Lichtman, R. 2012. *Liberal İdeolojinin Marksist Eleştirisi: Eleştirel Toplumsal Kuram Üzerine Denemeler.* İstanbul: Yordam Kitap.

Milanovic, B. 2019. *Capitalism, alone.* Cambridge, MA: Harvard University Press.

Mill, J. S. [1848]1965. *Principles of political economy. Collected Works. Vol. II–III.* Toronto: Toronto University Press.

———. [1843]1973. *A system of Logic Ratiocinative and Inductive*, ed. F. E. L. Priestly and J. M. Robson, Collected Works. Vol. *VII–VIII.* Toronto: Toronto University Press.

———. [1861]1977a. *Considerations on representative government*, ed. F. E. L. Priestly and J. M. Robson, Collected Works. vol. *XIX.* Toronto: Toronto University Press.

———. [1859]1977b. *On liberty*, ed. M. Robson, 213–310. *Collected Works. Vol. XIX.* Toronto: Toronto University Press.

———. [1836]2003. *On the definition of political economy; and on the method of investigation proper to it.* Collected Works. Vol. *IV.* 309–339. Toronto: Toronto University Press.

Mouchot, C. 2003. *Méthodologie Économique.* Paris: Éd. du Seuil.

Nationwide Economics. 2023. *How has the pandemic impacted inflation.* https://blog.nationwidefinancial.com/markets-economy/how-has-the-pandemic-impacted-inflation/.

Olson, M. 1965. *The logic of collective action.* Cambridge, MA: Harvard University Press.

Özveren, E. 2000. Capitalism and democracy at a crossroads: The civilizational dimension. *Journal of Evolutionary Economics* 10: 49–65. https://doi.org/10.1007/s001910050005.

Piketty, T. 2014. *Capitalism in the twenty-first century.* Cambridge, MA: Belknap Press.

Rode, M., and J.D. Gwartney. 2012. Does democratization facilitate economic liberalization? *European Journal of Political Economy* 28 (4): 607–619.

Rueschemeyer, D., E.H. Stephens, and J.D. Stephens. 1992. *Capitalist development and democracy.* Chicago: University of Chicago Press.

Şaylan, G. 1998. *Demokrasi ve Demokrasi Düşüncesinin Gelişmesi.* Ankara: Türkiye ve Orta Doğu Amme İdaresi Enstitüsü.

Schumpeter, J.A. 1908. *Das Wesen und der Hauptinhalt der theoretischen Nationalökonomie.* Munich and Leipzig: Duncker und Humblot.

———. 1909. On the concept of social value. *Quarterly Journal of Economics* 23 (2): 213–232.

———. 1954. *History of economic analysis.* Oxford: Oxford University Press.

Schumpeter, J. A. [1942]2008. *Capitalism, socialism and democracy.* New York: First Harper Perennial Thought Edition.

Skorupski, J. 2006. *Why read Mill today?* London and New York: Routledge.

Smith, A. [1776]1976. *An inquiry into the causes and nature of the Wealth of Nations.* Chicago: The University of Chicago Press.

Stigler, G.J. 1971. The theory of economic regulation. *Bell Journal of Economics and Management Science 2* (1): 3–21.

Toma, E.F. 2014. Public choice and public policy: A tribute to James Buchanan. *Southern Economic Journal* 80 (4): 892–897.

Tyler, C. 2006. Review article: Elitism and Anti-elitism in Nineteenth Century Democratic Thought. *History of European Ideas* 32 (3): 345–355.

Warner, Beth E. 2001. John Stuart Mill's theory of bureaucracy within representative government: Balancing competence and participation. *Public Administration Review* 61 (4): 403–413.

Weber, M. 1968. *Economy and society: An outline of interpretative sociology.* Vol. 1. New York: Bedminster Press.

Zouboulakis, M.S. 2002. John Stuart Mill's institutional individualism. *History of Economic Ideas* 10 (3): 29–45.

———. 2005. On the social nature of rationality in Adam Smith and John Stuart Mill. *Dans Cahiers d'économie Politique* 49: 51–63.

CHAPTER 2

# Capitalism, Democracy, and Elites Today

**Abstract** Since the beginning of the neoliberal era, it has been argued that there was a correlation between democracy and capitalism, and a strong democracy could ensure capitalist development and increase welfare. Thus, M. Friedman's (1912–2006) especially discussed democracy and capitalism as coexisting systems in *Capitalism and Freedom* ([1962]2002). This approach argued that a strong democracy would lead to capitalism, individual freedoms would be guaranteed under the capitalist system, and capitalist development would in turn lead to democratic development. However, the events of the twenty-first century demonstrated that capitalism was not a guarantor of individual freedoms and democracy as claimed by the liberals. The abovementioned correlation between capitalism and democracy became quite controversial after the crisis of 2008. In the affected countries, the crisis led to an increasing authoritarian trend. Public or state-driven corporations started to compete in international markets, leading to the emergence of an economic and political elite closely associated with politicians. Today, neoliberalism and state capitalism ensured security for the richest but increased the poverty and misery of most of the society. Increasing inequality made the consent on neoliberal policies unsustainable. This increased the conflict between democracy and liberalism as the states became increasingly authoritarian.



G. Baş Dinar, Ç. Akdere, *Tensions Between Capitalism and Democracy Today From the Perspective of J. S. Mill and J. A. Schumpeter*, https://doi.org/10.1007/978-3-031-45547-6_2

**Keywords** The crisis of capitalism • The crisis of democracy • Elites • Lobbies

Since the beginning of the neoliberal era, it has been argued that there was a correlation between democracy and capitalism, and a strong democracy could ensure capitalist development and increase welfare. Thus, M. Friedman's (1912–2006) especially discussed democracy and capitalism as coexisting systems in *Capitalism and Freedom* ([1962] 2002). This approach argued that a strong democracy would lead to capitalism, individual freedoms would be guaranteed under the capitalist system, and capitalist development would in turn lead to democratic development. However, the events of the twenty-first century demonstrated that capitalism was not a guarantor of individual freedoms and democracy as claimed by the liberals.

The abovementioned correlation between capitalism and democracy became quite controversial after the crisis of 2008. In the affected countries, the crisis led to an increasing authoritarian trend. Public or state-driven corporations started to compete in international markets, leading to the emergence of an economic and political elite closely associated with politicians. Today, neoliberalism ensured security for the richest but increased the poverty and misery of most of society. Increasing inequality made the consent on neoliberal policies unsustainable. This increased the conflict between democracy and liberalism as the states became increasingly authoritarian.

Democracy could be described as a regime where masses of ordinary people could actively participate in public life through debate and autonomous organizations. However, in a real democracy, citizens could participate actively in political debate and set the agenda. Although this is a difficult ideal to realize, it is valuable because it is the benchmark for democracy and also because democracy could be improved with this ideal (Crouch 2016, 12, 13). The current representative democracy reduced democracy to elections. J. A. Schumpeter (1883–1950) argued that democracy was a competitive arena for the leaders. Voters make their choices based on programs announced by the leaders and their parties. This is quite far from the ideal democracy. Voters do not set the political agenda but vote on the elected program. This leads to a formal democracy, which gradually deteriorates in essence. This democracy, where mass participation is limited by elections, leads to a government influenced by business lobbies, in other words, elites.

According to Crouch, the democratic expectations of the current liberal democracy are quite low and have created indifferent masses despite an environment called postdemocracy (Crouch 2016, 13). According to Crouch, although elections still exist in liberal democracies, the political debate during elections is firmly controlled by professionals on rival teams who specialize in persuasion techniques. The debates conducted during the elections are reduced to a set of questions chosen by these individuals. Most citizens adopt a rather passive and indifferent attitude. Citizens cannot set the topics of the political debate and only react to signals they receive. However, the real policies are determined during secret negotiations between the elected governments and the elites who predominantly represent the interests of the business owners. Thus, the conditions that Crouch defined as postdemocracy increase the power of business lobbies, prevent egalitarian policies, and limit the influence of powerful interest groups (Crouch 2016, 14).

## The Crisis of 2008 and Aftermath: From Capitalist Crisis to Democratic Crisis

Mainstream economists described the crisis of 2008 as a financial crisis in the US housing market and ultimately brought the financial markets to the brink of collapse; however, they failed to analyze the long-term and multidimensional elements behind the crisis. It was not accurate to describe the 2008 global crisis, the effects of which still endure, as a solely financial crisis. It should be approached with a structural and multidimensional analysis. Although the crisis erupted in unregulated global financial markets, it was only the tip of the iceberg. The crisis was an outcome of the long-term evolution of capital accumulation and stagnation of the capitalist global economy in the early 1970s. The crisis of 2008 was originally a continuation of the recession of the 1970s.

Thus, the analysis of the crisis of 2008 should begin with the evolution of the capitalist global economy between the 1929 Depression and the 1970s and should be based on the causes of the recession in the 1970s. As is known, the free market economy and the laissez-faire suffered a great loss in reputation after the 1929 Depression. Developed capitalist countries implemented certain policies to control and regulate the free market economy after the early 1930s. The efficiency of the market was weakened by certain policies, such as competitive limitations by political market interventions, implementation of capital controls and strict regulation of financial capital, implementation of fixed exchange rates and strong expansion of the public sector and the influence of the state.

The expansion of the state into the economy led to rapid and stable growth in advanced capitalist economies. Although there were periodic economic fluctuations in advanced capitalist economies in this period, governments alleviated the effects of the contraction with expansionary policies and prevented a general recession similar to the 1929 depression. It was determined that Keynesian policies built on *General Theory* ([1936] 1973) were the reason for the rapid economic growth in this period, and the Keynesian welfare state was used to describe this period. Although these policies contributed to economic growth, the economic success in this period could not be explained only by Keynesian policies. The stable and long growth was due to the combination of certain historical conditions that allowed the worldwide growth of capitalism (Savran 2013, 47, 49; Wahl 2015, 49).

In this period, one of the most important factors that promoted rapid capital accumulation was high profit rates. Due to the dissipation of fascism in Europe between the two world wars, authoritarian governments established significant control over the working class and suppressed real wages, leading to higher profits, productivity, and employment. Additionally, due to the efforts to redevelop the nations damaged by World War II, high demand for investment and consumption created the necessary conditions for rapid capital accumulation (Brenner 2015, 24). The Marshall Plan implemented by the US Secretary of State George Marshall allowed the transfer of approximately 12.7 billion dollars between 1948 and 1951, and 65% of the aid was transferred to industrialized nations such as the UK, France, Germany, and Italy. The American condition of promoting US foreign policies in exchange for aid led to the emergence of the USA as a global power (Türel 2017, 72–74). Furthermore, in exchange for Marshall Aid, the USA stipulated the export of mass production methods such as Fordism and Taylorism, which were only applied in the USA before World War II, to other capitalist countries, facilitating production and increasing manufacturing efficiency and productivity

(Curtis 2015, 92). Fordism weakened the impact of fluctuations in capitalist countries via the globalization of cheap raw material supply (Harvey 2014, 160).

Furthermore, the Bretton Woods agreement (1944) indexed all national currencies to the US dollar, declaring the dollar a global currency. The presence of a common currency led to a stable world trade and capital flow, strengthening the role of the USA as a global power. Another factor that led to rapid economic growth after World War II was the economic relations established between developed nations and those that acquired political independence after the war. The former used the latter as a source of cheap labor and raw material, transferring the added value created in these countries to developed nations. Additionally, GATT and Kennedy Round agreements allowed the liberalization of trade between imperialist countries after World War II (Savran 2013, 54–55). These historical developments led to the rapid expansion of the global market and increased specialization, and the conditions favored rapid capital accumulation.

The abovementioned historical developments led to the acceleration of capital accumulation, and the increase in labor demand strengthened the position of the working class. As the workers became stronger, labor unions became stronger and demanded certain rights that allowed them to gain benefits such as sick leave, accident leave, and retirement (Baş Dinar 2022, 152). These developments were the outcome of the class struggle waged by the working class against the exploitation and social insecurity imposed by capitalism. Thus, the welfare state was based on the collaboration between labor and capital. Thus, the welfare state practices adopted during the 30 years that followed World War II led to significant improvements in the living standards of the working class. The welfare state regulations resolved the conflict between the workers and the capitalists peacefully based on a legal framework (Wahl 2015, 54–57).

The welfare state policies and the rapid economic growth in the post-World War II era led to a strong correlation between capitalism and democracy. The increase in the welfare of the working class and capital accumulation contributed to the idea that capitalism was an ideal system not only for the interests of the property owners but also for the working class. In this period, the idea that capitalism was good for not only a group of property-owner privileged classes but also for the interests of the masses, and in that sense, that it was democratic, became prominent.

However, the decrease in profits after the mid-1960s indicated that the period of welfare had come to an end. In 1974, OPEC increased oil prices, leading to a major crisis. The 1974 crisis was an economic turning point, and welfare state policies started to be questioned. To reestablish profitability, the benefits of the working class acquired during the democratic capitalism period should be reduced after the crisis. These years witnessed a serious paradigm shift and a new era of neoliberalism in economic theory and policy. Neoliberalism could be described as a strategy that aimed to restore profitability through privatization, deregulation, flexibility, weakening of social benefits, and deunionization (Savran 2013, 37).

Furthermore, the globalization strategy adopted by international economic institutions allowed the implementation of neoliberal policies globally. Globalization strategies were implemented with the liberalization of capital and commodity movements. Financial liberalization allowed the development of new financial instruments and an extraordinary increase in global financial activities. The financial system altered the balance of power in global capitalism and led to a greater autonomy of the banking and finance industries against large companies, states, and individuals. As this process provided greater opportunities for the financial system to spread risks, it also created an environment susceptible to currency and financial crises. In this period, the globalization of financial capital led to a significant decrease in the ability of nation states to control the capital flow and implement monetary and fiscal policies. After the collapse of the Bretton Woods System in 1971 and the adoption of the flexible exchange rate system in 1973, financial capital began to determine domestic policies in all nation states (Harvey 2014, 188–190). After globalization, the nation state was no longer the organization tool of capitalism, and nation states tended to serve global interest groups instead of the national accumulation of wealth (Freeman and Kagartlitsky 2007, 12). With the collapse of the welfare state, the association between capitalism and democracy weakened.

The crisis in 1974 led to the criticism of the Keynesian welfare state. To end the economic recession and increase profits, liberalism was revived. Francis Fukuyama argued that the fall of the Berlin Wall marked the end of history and the collapse of the socialist system in 1989, and alternatives to Western liberalism were completely exhausted and capitalism remained the only alternative (Fukuyama 1989). This idea, which was immediately accepted by the liberals, provided ideological legitimacy to neoliberal policies, and free market economy and liberal democracy were considered the sole solution for economic and political problems. Thus, the globalists declared the undisputed dominance of the free market economy with the slogan "there is no alternative" (Baş Dinar 2022, 157).

After the 1980s, Third World countries were pressured to remove trade and financial barriers to inclusion in the global economy. Thus, the Third World Countries, which gained their political independence after World War II, became dependent on developed capitalist economies. International institutions such as the World Bank, International Monetary Fund and World Trade Organization pressured these nations to implement a series of neoliberal policies such as the reduction of social assistance, privatization of health and education, and liberalization of commodity and capital flows, leading to significant profits for international capital in these countries via direct and speculative capital investments (Pröbristing 2011, 96). Thus, the achievements of the working class during the post-World War II period were shelved with the excuse that they disrupted market functions. Furthermore, the privatization of public enterprises led to new sources of profit for capital and reduced the unionization and political power of the working class (Savran 2013, 85–87).

Despite neoliberal policies, the real market stagnation that started in the 1970s could not be eliminated, and the greed for more profit in financial markets led to a shift in the focus of capitalists from real markets to financial markets during the 1980s and 1990s. In the late 1990s, liberalization and neoliberal policies led to financial product diversity and credit expansion. Financial markets no longer conducted their main functions, and the finance industry became independent from manufacturing industries, leading to a debt-initiated speculative expansion and laying the groundwork for the crisis of 2008 (Panitch and Gindin 2012, 25). To resolve the chronic stagnation experienced in the world economy since the 1970s, neoliberal policies, globalization, and financialization strategies were implemented. However, although these strategies contributed to the partial recovery of the UK and US economies between 1993 and 2007, they were not a permanent solution to stagnation (Brenner 2011, 211). Curtis (2015) likened the financialization of the economy to the treatment of stagnation inherent in mature capitalism with a band aid (Curtis 2015, 88).

Neoliberal policies implemented to eradicate recession reinforced it by oppressing labor and reducing wages and purchasing power. Financialization and globalization temporarily helped overcome this neoliberalist contradiction. Financialization facilitated household, corporate, and public loans, balancing the constriction of demand in neoliberalism.

Thus, the borrowing opportunities introduced by financialization led to an increase in consumption despite the continuous decrease in real wages.

Although neoliberal ideology advocated the reduction of the role of the state in economic affairs and the dominance of the free market economy, neoliberal policies required comprehensive intervention of the state in economic, social, and political affairs. After the 1970s, the states became oppressive in implementing neoliberal policies despite the reaction of the poor working class. The relationship between liberalism and the state has been contradictory since its inception. As indicated by Polanyi, for the development of the market and market economy, government intervention that imposed a market order was required when needed (Polanyi 2008, 333).

At its core, neoliberalism aims to change the distribution of income to favor capital. This means redistribution of income from the poor working masses to capitalist classes. After the 1970s, corporations demanded further tax exemptions and reductions, and states had to invest more in infrastructure to facilitate private sector investments. To meet these investor demands, low and middle income groups were taxed more by raising consumption taxes and social security payments. Furthermore, since the democratic order was in decline due to the decrease in the participation of the electorate and the power of the unions and political parties, this led to the reorganization of the distribution of income to favor the capital, in other words, the transfer of income from the low-income classes to the higher-income classes (Streeck 2016, 17–22).

In the neoliberal era, the state played an active role in the redistribution of income and wealth in favor of the capitalist classes and creating conditions for primary accumulation conditions by transferring public resources to the private sector. Through privatization, the state eliminated the bottlenecks in accumulation by developing new profits by marketing public assets (Harvey 2008, 131). Thus, neoliberalism could be described as a political project that aimed to establish the conditions for capital accumulation (Harvey 2015, 27).

In the neoliberal era, state intervention in the redistribution that favored capital refuted the neoliberal thesis that the market economy would improve democracy and devastate authoritarian regimes. In contrast, neoliberal policies significantly damaged democracy by reducing accountability, pluralism, and national sovereignty in important domains. Furthermore, globalization that ensured the implementation of neoliberalist policies globally led to the prioritization of the demands of international corporations and significantly limited the implementation of national policies. The threat of international investors withdrawing their investments from a country became a significant obstacle to the expansion of the national economy and implementation of economic and social policies that would remedy income distribution. Furthermore, the frequent financial crises in the neoliberal era were among the factors that increased the power of international institutions such as the IMF over nation states. The IMF, which prioritized the interests of global financial circles, provided financial aid to developing countries to end the crisis in exchange for the implementation of neoliberal policies (Chang and Grabel 2005, 39–41). This caused significant damage to nation-state democracies by reducing national sovereignty in economic and political policies that were demanded by their citizens.

Crouch (2016) described this period as when minority interests were prioritized and democracy declined as postdemocracy. This period was characterized by politicians who acted like merchants and a decrease in respect for political professions. Crouch compared politicians with shopkeepers who had to constantly compete to stay in business and try to determine the desires of their customers (Crouch 2016, 28). The current reduction in political participation in elections and the transformation of elections into marketing due to competition between political parties emptied the political domain. The reduction of the elections into marketing activities led to a need for large financial resources in elections, similar to the USA, and political parties required financing by corporations and wealthy interest groups. In addition, political authority had to submit to the demands of the interest groups that supported them rather than the demands of the people to be elected. Governments had to consider the demands of these interest groups in important political decisions. Furthermore, the reduction of politics into marketing and the shrouded political agenda of the parties manipulated and pacified the voters, reducing their participation in political decision-making (Crouch 2016, 28).

However, this did not mean that democracy has completely vanished. According to Crouch, although the formal components of democracy continued to exist in postdemocracy, the political participation of the masses was quite low. In this period, where welfare state achievements were minimized, unions were marginalized, inequality increased, the redistribution function of taxation was lost, politicians had to submit to the interests of certain capital owners, the poor became indifferent to their status, their interest in politics became extremely low, and democracy entered a period of significant decline. Behind these elements, which Crouch described as postdemocracy, lied the increasing power of global corporations and their influence over political decisions. Global neoliberal policies gradually reduced the impact of working class organizations and created weak, unorganized, and politically passive masses. Furthermore, the collapse of Keynesianism and mass production led to a decrease in economic significance, hence decreasing the political power of the masses (Crouch 2016, 35).

This was quite similar to the politician described by Schumpeter ([1942] 2008) in his competitive democracy model. Today, politics is significantly competitive, as indicated by Schumpeter. Political parties manipulate the masses with business and marketing methods to get elected rather than discussing party programs. Thus, party programs and the concrete political goals are not discussed much. Here, the liberal prediction that competition and a free market would always produce effective results should be discussed. As indicated by Schumpeter, as economic competition is imperfect in the capitalist system and inevitably threatens the future of capitalism by leading to monopolies in the long run, political competition harms democracy. It could be suggested that the competition between political parties or politicians does not bring about a better democracy but converts politics and elections into lobbying, increasing the power of economic elites when compared to politicians, and leading to anti-democratic practices, as discussed in the next section.

## The Rise of Lobbying and the Increasing Power of Elites

As mentioned in the previous section, the neoliberal policies implemented after the recession of the real markets in the early 1970s increased the pressure of competition on corporations. Keynesian welfare state policies could guarantee aggregate demand and relatively stable profitability. After the end of the Keynesian welfare state, the lack of this guarantee and the increase in global competition due to rapid technological advances increased the demands of global conglomerates. They threatened to leave a country when they were not happy with the monetary regime of the country or labor market regulations, increasing their impact on government decisions. The demands of global corporations shifted the tax burden from corporations to individuals, negatively affecting income distribution and public financing (Crouch 2016, 38, 39).

D. Acemoğlu and J. Robinson (2020) also argued that both political and economic institutions and resources were controlled by elites. They argued that these two powers strengthened one another (Acemoğlu and Robinson 2020, 441, 442; Milanoviç 2019). An analysis of the relations between political and economic elites is required to better understand this process and to reverse the inequality of opportunity and income. Thus, the elites who hold economic power would begin to "capture" the legislature, a case that J. Stigler (1971) did not recognize in regulatory capture theory. As stated by G. Kolko (1963 cited by Holcombe, 2016), it would not be possible to establish an egalitarian economic and political order in that case. The elites would organize the regulations to strengthen their stance and prevent their opponents from hindering or disrupting this position.

One of the most important studies that discussed the role of the ruling elite in contemporary society was written by C. W. Mills (1916–1962). Mills, in *Power Elite*, first published in 1956, argued that the power elite included individuals with different properties and powers when compared to ordinary people due to their privileges and knowledge of life. These people could have a great impact on society and make decisions that lead to important consequences. In his work, where he approached the power of the said elites in American society, Mills investigated three major institutions, namely, the state hierarchy, the corporate hierarchy, and the military hierarchy. He concluded that these were the most important power instruments in American society. Mills argued that these tools of power were held by financial elites (Mills [1956] 2000).

There has been a correlation between the increasing influence of global corporations on governments and the decline of democracy in the twenty-first century. Today, policies are determined by a group of elites, similar to the pre-democratic era. As emphasized by Crouch (2016), this has sometimes been in the form of external pressures applied to governments and sometimes due to changes in political parties. In both cases, the process undermined democracy by increasing the dominance of the economic elites over the government. Behind this process, which Crouch called postdemocracy, was the growing political power of the corporations. According to Crouch, the way to preserve capitalist dynamics and return from postdemocracy was to find the political tools that would prevent the political influence of corporate executives. Furthermore, Crouch (2016) argued that global financial capitalism should be limited to reconcile democratic principles and capitalism, similar to the mid-twentieth century. Crouch strongly objected to the argument that unrestricted liberalism theoretically leads to a perfect market. According to Crouch, the currently adopted policies serve the interests of large corporations and create new oligarchies (Crouch 2016, 102–3).

The role of elites in democracy has been a significant historical debate. The term elite, which was derived from the Latin "eligra" and "electa", meaning "elected", has been prevalent since the seventeenth century. The term became prevalent in social sciences in the late nineteenth century (Arslan 2007, 2). In the twentieth century, the works of V. Pareto (1848–1923) and G. Mosca (1858–1941) led to an increased interest in elites in social sciences. According to Pareto, society consists of two layers, elites and non-elites. Pareto described elites as those who belong to a class of people with the highest standards in their fields and divided them into ruling elites and non-ruling elites. Ruling elites played a direct or indirect key role in the government, while the non-ruling elites were privileged individuals in society with a weaker influence on the government (Pareto 1935, 1421–1423). Similarly, Mosca argued that society included two classes: the rulers and the ruled. The rulers, albeit few, led social power and enjoyed the privileges of power. The rest of the society was coercively ruled and controlled by the former class, either legitimately or arbitrarily. Mosca emphasized that the ruling minority had significant traits with a significant impact on society (Mosca 1939).

Later studies on elites discussed the arguments of Pareto and Mosca. These studies on the ruling elite inevitably led to a discussion on the relationship between democracy and elites. Several studies in the literature have argued that the government of society by the elite contradicts the idea of democracy. According to Bottomore (1996), this contradiction was due to two factors. First, the prioritization of the inequality between individual talents by elite theories is intrinsically opposed to democratic political ideals, which emphasize the fundamental equality of individuals. Second, the idea of government by a ruling minority contradicted the democratic notion of the rule of the majority. However, Bottomore (1996) indicated that this contradiction was not as clear and significant as it might seem. In the democratic political system, "rule by the people", in other words, "de facto rule of the majority", was impossible in practice. Democracy could be translated as the principle of the openness of the government to all. Thus, there will be a constant struggle to obtain or sustain the government (Bottomore 1996, 15, 16).

According to Iversen and Soskice (2019, 134–140), it would not be accurate to perceive elites as a new class; in contrast, there has always been a conflict between "industrializing or modernizing elites" and "landowner elites". Landed elites "played a substantial role at the local level, where they controlled local councils alone" (Iversen and Soskice 2019, 140). Examples of this could be observed in England and France, where there is a distinction between landed and urban elites. However, today, another type of elite has emerged: industrializing elites. Industrializing elites hold the power to determine the course of both capitalism and democracy. As mentioned by Acemoglu and Robinson and Boix (cited by Iversen and Soskice 2019, 115), "*industrializing elites granted democracy to counter the power of the conservative forces that opposed industrialization*". This power of the industrializing elites was not based on the pressure of the working class, as suggested by power resource theory.

Indeed, "a large unified labor movement that demanded democracy emerged" (Iversen and Soskice 2019, 109), but during the democratic struggle, elites were also very active and determinative besides the workers in nondemocratic advanced capitalist states, especially in the United States and the UK, as well as Australia, New Zealand, and Canada (Collier 1999 in Iversen and Soskice 2019, 85). In the UK, "skilled workers were introduced into the class of decisive voters, diminishing the role of landowners in the House of Lords and other upper houses, as well as in local governments", and in the United States, "the Republican ascendency of the late nineteenth century in effect allowed the survival of the conservative plantation-owners in Southern states, hostile to industrialization." This was the story of the development of advanced capitalism in the North (Iversen and Soskice 2019, 102–103).

In *Capital in the Twenty-First Century*, published in French in 2013 and popularized after it was published in English in 2014, T. Piketty argued that the biggest problem of twenty-first century capitalism was inequality. The book became extremely popular since it approached inequality based on a historical and theoretical analysis and argued that this development threatened the future of capitalism and democracy. The problem of inequality has increased dramatically in the twenty-first century and became one of the most emphasized issues in the "Occupy Wall Street" protests, which were initiated in New York on September 17, 2011, and then spread rapidly to the whole USA and the rest of the world.

During these protests, the activists emphasized the exploitation of the 99% by the top 1% and underlined the increase in injustice and poverty due to the distribution of income (Baş Dinar 2015, 17).

The most important issue that Piketty discussed in the book was the acquisition of inequality through inheritance and rent. Piketty indicated that inequality was rooted in the ideal of a society based only on merit and effort in contemporary democratic society and argued that the rise of the rentier class would seriously harm democracy. According to Piketty, there was a serious conflict between the equality of rights for all citizens in democracy and the inequality in the living conditions of the people. Piketty emphasized that to overcome this conflict, social inequalities should be based on rational and universal factors. Piketty indicated that the association between economic and technological rationality and democracy was weak. He seriously questioned the correlation between capitalism and democracy, noting that true democracy and social justice required specific institutions, not the institutions of the market. The idea that free competition would reduce inequality and lead to a more democratic world was a dangerous illusion according to Piketty (Piketty 2015, 457).

Formal democracy, that is, the equality of citizens before the law, does not necessitate a democratic society. Democracy is more than a formal system founded on equality before the law. Although formal freedoms still exist, as claimed by Piketty, de facto inequality induced by capitalist society was an obstacle to real democracy. According to Crouch (2016), democracy requires a certain degree of equality since it entails the impact of all citizens on political decisions. In contrast, liberalism required various opportunities to influence these decisions. These were correlated and mutually dependent conditions. According to Crouch, the ideal democracy could not thrive without strong liberalism. However, Crouch indicated that these two were different and that there was a conflict between liberalism and democracy. Thus, the higher the political equality is, the stronger the possibility of developing rules and constraints to reduce inequality. This contradicted the freedom that liberal philosophers demanded for political action (Crouch 2016, 24).

The 1990–2014 dataset on elite and business world relations demonstrated the hegemony of transnational capital (Scheiring 2020). This hegemony raised the following question: "Do the 'right' type of politicians have the skills and the will to strike the necessary pacts with the elites and establish the 'right' type of institutions?" (O'Donnell and Schmitter, 1986 cited by Scheiring 2020, 3). The best way to understand who the contemporary elites are is the definition by Mills in *The Power Elite* ([1956] 2000). Mills began with Jacob Burckhardt's short definition: "They are all that we are not". In fact, they were those who made decisions with major consequences, who governed the military establishment, who occupied the strategic command posts of the society, they were the advisers and consultants. They were the spokespeople and opinion-makers. They were the captains of their own ideas and decisions. They held the power of influential instruments of wealth. Thus, where do government officials or politicians fit in this group? He continued, "Immediately below the elite are the professional politicians of the middle levels of power, in the Congress and in the pressure groups, as well as among the new and old upper classes in towns, cities and regions" (Mills [1956] 2000, 4).

Mills openly argued that during the "material boom, a nationalist celebration, a political vacuum" in American society, elites were an important interest group and therefore a power group and theorized this approach (Wolfe [1956] 2000). This discussion revolved around a previously proposed topic: "a meritocratic society governed by a plurality of separate elites". According to Mills, countries were ruled by a single elite power, and this power was manifested through private schools, elite universities, private clubs, and the marriage market (Gusterson 2015, 387).

Crouch (2016) illustrated this with the example of party financing in American democracy. The parties sponsored by wealthy interest groups would have a greater advantage in winning the elections unless the aid of the donors is limited. Crouch argued that this power, while compatible with the principles of liberalism, would undermine democracy. Because the election race would not be equal for all parties. Instead, public financing, limits on election campaign expenditures and TV ads could contribute to democracy and relative equality. However, he argued that this would also sacrifice freedoms (Crouch 2016, 24).

On the other hand, in this debate, another concept was proposed by those who associated the concept with the current times: financial elites (Gusterson 2015). According to Hartmann (2015, 396), "*top politicians and executives, as well as outstanding athletes or scientists are considered elite*". This was investigated based on the lifestyle of financial elites, elite taste cultures, and the world of scientific elites, who were described as bankers and financial traders by ethnographers and lived in regions with high digital technology penetration. These studies argued that the global capitalist order was "*increasingly financialized, dependent on a burgeoning new class of knowledge producers, and marked by social and economic inequality*" that was not seen in the West for a very long time (Castells 2009; Gouldner 1979; Harvey 2007; Piketty 2014 cited by Gusterson 2015, 388).

In *Giants: The Global Power Elite* (2018), Phillips argued that Mills followed the footsteps of 'the theory of *The Power Elite*, introduced in 1956, and F. Hunter's study of community power in Atlanta, *Community Power Structure: A Study of Decision Makers* (1953). The power was not in individuals, mainstream political science, or the social classes as argued by Marxism but in organizations, voluntary associations, interest groups, and parties that facilitate industrialization. The previous power elite generation was active in national corporate and political networks. In the age of globalism, that generation became obsolete, and "national capitalist classes developed via the integration of their capital into a transnational capitalist class" (Phillips 2018). Financial giants (BlackRock, Vanguard, J. P. Morgan Chase, to Morgan Stanley & Co.) and their investment partners formed the elites called "*New Giants*" and "*Near Giants*" (Phillips 2018, 37–49). These had more than one trillion dollars in assets and symbiotically invested in each other as of 2017.

The complex, bureaucratized and marketized structure of the society differentiated the elites with the inclusion of physicists, investment lawyers, etc. Industrialized society meant the presence of diverse elites. The power of these modern elites gradually increased and became associated with the bureaucracy, investment banks, and education system, while traditional elites were still determined by ancestry and kinship (Gusterson 2015). As emphasized by Crouch, the environment where lobbies and vested interests determine policies is far from democratic. The influence of lobbies and interest groups, which could be described as elites, on the government, is higher than that on the masses. First and foremost, business lobbies could threaten with failure if the government ignores their demands. This threat is extremely effective on the government since economic success is one of the most fundamental concerns of any government. Additionally, lobbying is an important investment that would provide high profits. Thus, these circles allocate significant resources to these activities. However, the masses could threaten the economic success of governments. They also do not have the economic resources to pressure the government (Crouch 2016, 25).

The increasing significance of global corporations in the global economy and their effects on government decisions concentrated the power and wealth of these corporations. The power of senior executives is unlimited in most of these corporations. The chief executive officer (CEO) in the Anglo-American corporate model holds all the responsibility and authority. Since the model is almost universal after globalization, Crouch argued that corporate managers have acquired significant power over governments. Delegation of corporate management to these people, as well as individuals, means that they directly affect government decisions (Crouch 2016, 44, 45).

Thus, this means that a new elite class monopolized economic and social life, similar to the pre-democratic era. Today, the dependence of global corporate executives on political parties and the government and the dependence of political parties and the government on the economic resources of these corporations have led to a new oligarchic system. The enormous income and power of corporate executives have been debated since the crisis of 2008. This corporate structure led to a more unequal distribution of wealth in the society, and inequality strengthened these individuals and their control over the governments.

## Who Are the Elites?

Who are the elites? Do they constitute social class? Do they have similar interests in constituting a social group?

Analysis of the elites was developed as an opposition to Marxist class analysis in Europe during the late nineteenth century. The main objection by elite theorists was the Marxist division of society into classes as those that control or do not control the means of production and the Marxist approach that focused on the conflict between these classes as the key to understanding social evolution. Elite theorists emphasized that privileged individuals played a key role in the government instead of social classes. Thus, they discussed the government by elites rather than the intraclass conflicts and the decisions of privileged individuals who governed the entire population. Ruling elites play significant roles in the comprehension of social change. In other words, the problem of social evolution that Marx and other philosophers focused on was examined based on the behavior of the ruling elites.

Kahan (1992, 5) reported that 'aristos' in Greek and the humanist etymology of aristocracy, the 'elite,' means the 'best' semantically. 'Elite' reflects a certain common repugnance toward the masses and middle classes. In the classical era, it was characterized by common values and tastes; thus, there was no classification of the elites. In the modern era, especially with the introduction of nineteenth-century educational systems, namely, English public schools, French lycées, and German gymnasiums, cultural penetration was successful until World War I (Kahan 1992, 82).

Plato (c. 380–360 B.C.E.) first introduced the concept of ruling elites and coined them "philosopher kings" (kings of a hive, better and more perfectly educated than the rest) in *Republic volume VII*. Italian diplomat N. Machiavelli (1469–1527) employed the terms noble, 'aristocrat,' or 'the great' to describe social elites. H. de Saint-Simon (1760–1825) separated the traditional and modern elites during the French Revolution. On one side was the landowner aristocracy, and on the other was the "entrepreneurs, financiers, and scholars—people whose importance derived from their functions rather than status". The term 'elite' was published in the Encyclopédie between 1751 and 1772 and described as "exquisite, top-of-the-line products, while its meaning was later extended to designate membership in a superior social group (*'hommes d 'élite'*)" (Korom 2015, 390).

Elites have not been adequately studied and theorized in social sciences. This was due to the ambiguity of the term. It stemmed from the dual use of the term: traditional and modern elites. The privileges of political and economic elites differ. These factors include genealogy, land ownership, control of capital, bureaucratic office, educational achievements, or religious status. For some, 'elite' means the 'ruling class', while it means something more contextual for others, revealing that every class or group has an elite stratum, such as 'skilled workers' in the working class. Subsequent studies emphasized that perceptions about colonialism and capitalism have changed the semantics of the term. This new semantics included factors such as access to capital, education, and bureaucratic privileges. In other words, "while bureaucratic industrial societies presented themselves as meritocracies, elites devised strategies hereditarily dependent on their privileged access to the educational system and cultural capital" (Gusterson 2015, 386).

What is the difference between the "ruling class" and "elites"? Pareto called the ruling class and the ruling or governing elites what Mosca called the ruling class. According Hartman (2015, 397) "the elite rules due to its superior material and organizational possibilities as well as to its intellectual capabilities and by use of force."

This term was introduced to social sciences in the late nineteenth century (Korom 2015). Gustave Le Bon's (1841–1931) work on the psychology of the masses (1895) was highly influential. According to Le Bon, the masses could not produce culture; only small, intellectual superior aristocrats could (Hartmann 2015, 397). Social psychologist Gustave Le Bon's *Das Gesetz der Macht* (The Law of Power) asserted that the ultimate power elite could conquer the minds of the people (Wieser 1926 in Kurz 2018). According to Le Bon, "internal powers" were more important than "outside forces". The relations between social elites and the masses depend on "internal powers" (Kurz 2018).

Philosophers who contributed to elite theory, including Pareto (1916, 1935), Mosca (1939) and R. Michels (1999), sought to develop an alternative to Marxist theory. Pareto investigated European elites and questioned whether there was "a meritocratic basis for social stratification". However, the studies of these two authors did not raise the interest of anthropologists (Gusterson 2015).

It was first mentioned in *Trattato di sociologia generale 1915–19* (A General Sociology Treatise) by Italian economist Pareto, who dedicated his life to sociology after his significant contributions to economics. However, the term has been used to mean 'fewness' and 'excellence' by K. Mannheim (1940), R. Dahrendorf (1962; 1972), R. A. Dahl (2005), and S. Keller (1991), who developed pluralist elite theory. J. Ortega y Gasset (1929/1957) employed dichotomies such as 'noble man' versus 'mass man' to clarify the meaning of the term. Finally, the term was accepted to mean "the rule of the minority over the majority of the population" (Korom 2015, 394).

Anthropologists ignored the issue of elites in their analysis of Western societies in the 1950s and 1960s. Then, an important debate started between sociologists and intellectuals after the publication of *The Power Elite* by Mills. Mills ([1956] 2000), 301) cited Mill; however, it was not clear what he meant: "How much the cogency of the classic view of the public rested upon a restriction of this public to the carefully educated is revealed by the fact that by 1859 even J. S. Mill (1806–1873) was writing of 'the tyranny of the majority,' and both Tocqueville and Burckhardt anticipated the view popularized recently by political moralists such as Ortega y Gasset." However, Mills was the one who introduced the concept of power elite in the nineteenth century, and this had to be included in the book.

Empirical studies have also been conducted on elites. Studies conducted in the 1960s and 1970s demonstrated that parental heritage, land ownership and craftsmanship were not quite important, but small and medium enterprises were important. Based on the research of the time, D. La Vere Bates (1973) wrote, "almost half of the [business] elite share similar occupational origins associated with commerce. It is significant that 77 percent of the elites shared two occupational origins: small- and medium-size commercial business owners, business executives, and government employees" (La Vere Bates 1973 in Bugra 1994, 59). The study was conducted with 103 businessmen, and the fathers of 35 held various public sector jobs; the fathers of 25 were small business owners. In these studies, it was determined that in a developing country such as Turkey, 79% of the business elite were college graduates. It was observed that 60% of these had an undergraduate degree, 14% had a master's degree, and 5% had a PhD. In other words, less than 25% of the elites did not have a college degree. All contributed significantly to the development and transformation of the country (Bugra 1994, 59).

Studies on elites were revived only after the 1970s, with the diversification of capitalism and the emergence of various types of democracy. In this period, mainly the differences between democracies were discussed. M. G. Burton and J. Higley attempted to understand the sources (1987) and transformations of elites (2001), while J. Pakulski (2012) took a different path and tried to conduct a Weberian interpretation of the elite theories. At the end of the Cold War, the elites in semi-democratic and authoritarian regimes were investigated (Svolik 2009; Zuba 2016 in Bilir and Şahin 2021). Hardly any of these studies cited the Millian approach to the elites. This was a huge miss. One of the aims of the present book was to fill this gap.

Various types of elites were described. The main groups of elites included the bureaucratic elite, Islamic elite, intellectual elite, political elite, and ruling elite. Some were synonymous. Hartmann (2015, 396) clarified the issue as follows:

> Classical elite theories assumed an unavoidable opposition of ruling elite and dominated masses; functionalist elite theories assumed competing performances and sectoral elites; critical elite theories identified power elites who were recruited based on social origin. Current elite literature discussed mostly the homogeneity of elites, the role they played in the increasingly unequal distribution of income, and their international property.

Elite theories assumed that a minority administration would develop and rule the majority. Thus, they argued that democracy and elites could never "reconcile". Keller (1991 in Korom 2015, 392) called this minority "strategic elites", who held high positions in various industries.

Wiesser derived a universal law he coined the "law of small numbers", which argued that a small number of people enjoyed power. The power of the elites lies in the control of people's minds and trust of their followers. This was the social domination of the elite (Wieser 1910, 12 in Kurz 2018). Although Wiesser was firmly attached to methodological individualism, he expanded the boundaries of administration and "rejected, the idea that the preferences of agents were given and immutable," and "instead insisted that they were endogenous and at least partially determined by political and economic leaders." He questioned whether those who rule under the influence of individuals also simply pursued their interests: "Similar to political leaders, they are often concerned with maximizing the number of their followers, that is, their clients and customers, and establishing a business empire or dynasty." (Both views resonated in the works of his former student Schumpeter) (Kurz 2018).

Different elite concepts were discussed in the book. "Managers" (Chap. 3) included 199 managers employed 17 asset management firms (Phillips 2018, 148), and "facilitators" (Chap. 4) "served as institutionalized mechanisms to build TCC consensus and power elites" (Phillips 2018, 161). These included certain IGOs (intergovernmental organizations), the World Bank, IMF, G30, G20, G7, WTO, World Economic Forum, Trilateral Commission, Bilderberg Group, Aspen Institute, Council on Foreign Relations (CFR), and Bank for International Settlements. "Facilitators" try to transfer the TCC power elite into a social class. "Protectors" (Chap. 5), or The Power Elite and the US Military, NATO Empire, Intelligence Agencies, and Private Military Companies, protect themselves and the elites with their law enforcement forces. "Ideologists" (Chap. 6) include corporate media and public relations companies and democratic developments.

Phillips (2018) approached the topic based on power structure theory and asked the following: "Are global power networks corrosive tools for privileged individuals and groups, or necessary adjuncts to finance, trade, and diplomacy?" "Industrial elite", "globalized power elite", and "Transnationalist Capitalist Class" (TCC) are different names of the same interest group. Power structure theory has existed for 20 years (Phillips, 2018, 9). These terms intended to identify national and global elites in resources, communication, trade, banking, economies, environment, government, etc., that "function as a nongovernmental network of similarly educated wealthy individuals with common interests in managing, facilitating, and protecting accumulated global wealth and insuring continuous growth of capital" (Phillips 2018, 9).

How could one define the power of elites? T. Piketty (2014, 29, 65, 99, 100, 180, 187, 193, 224, 241, 260, 279, 288, 292, 294–297, 339, 351, 400) introduced the concept of "global financial elites" to describe this power. He described this social group as "superelites" (182). This is "numerically quite large groups who inevitably stand out in society, especially when the individuals included in them tend to live in the same cities and even to congregate in the same neighborhoods. In every country the upper centile occupies a prominent place in the social landscape and not just in the income distribution" (Piketty 2014, 182). "Market power" is acquired by the financial elite and the "lobbies" they created with their inherited wealth. Thus, elites also acquired political power and "formed an oligopolistic structure in certain industries via systematic deregulations" (Bocutoğlu 2021, 5). Proving this was not easy. As argued by Bocutoğlu (2016), "market power and its natural result, 'economic power', used to influence political elections'. It was claimed that the financial elite was influential on regulatory institutions such as the US Treasury, the Fed, the US Securities and Exchange Commission (SEC), and policy implementation institutions such as the Credit Rating Agencies, Libor, IMF, and World Bank; however, this influence was hidden behind higher education institutions, foundations, think tanks and the media (Bocutoğlu 2016). Thus, an oligopolistic structure and imperfectly competitive markets were dominant in several industries, leading to the labor-capital imbalance (Bocutoğlu 2016). As argued by Brown (2007 in Spash 2017), "the power of money creation and leveraging allowed the elites to amass wealth at the expense of the masses. Empirical evidence on the accumulation of wealth and power and its harmful social effects is well known" (e.g., Stiglitz 2011; Piketty 2014 cited by Spash 2017).

## References

Acemoğlu, R., and J. A. Robinson. 2020. *Dar Koridor: Devletler, Toplumlar ve Özgürlüğün Geleceği*. Translated by Yüksel Taşkın. İstanbul: Doğan Kitap.

Arslan, A. 2007. *Elit Sosyolojisi*. Ankara: Phoenix Yayınları.

Baş Dinar, G. 2015. İktisadi Düşüncenin İzleğinde Piketty'i Değerlendirmek. *Ekonomik Yaklaşım* 26 (96): 15–41.

———. 2022. Devlet Kapitalizmini Anlamak: Deneyimler ve Tartışmalar. In *Devlet Kapitalizmi: Tarihsel Süreç, Kuramsal Tartışmalar ve Uygulamalar*, ed. G. Baş Dinar and S. Durusoy, 139–167. Ankara: Siyasal Kitabevi.

Bilir, H., and M. Şahin. 2021. Politik Ekonomiye Schumpeterci Bir Bakış: Kapitalizm Ve Siyasi Elitler. *Pamukkale Üniversitesi Sosyal Bilimler Enstitüsü Dergisi* 43: 263–276.

Bocutoğlu, E. 2016. Piketty'nin İkiz Günahı: Gelir ve Servet dağılımı Meselesini Tekrar İktisadi Analizin Merkezine Yerleştirmek ve Küresel Servet Vergisi Önermek. *Hak İş Uluslararası Emek ve Toplum Dergisi* 5 (12): 30–53.

———. 2021. Küresel Finansal Elit, Ana Akım İktisat ve Ana Akım Dışı İktisat (Global Financial Elite, Mainstream Economics and Non-Mainstream Economics). *Fiscaoeconomia* 5 (1): 1–20.

Bottomore, T. B. 1996. *Seçkinler ve Toplum*. Translated by Erol Mutlu. İstanbul: Gündoğan Yayınları.

Brenner, R. 2011. Küreselleşme ve Yeni Uzun Dalga Efsanesi. In *Marksist Kriz Teorisi ve Kredi Krizi*, ed. R. Brenner and M. Pröbristing, 171–217. İstanbul: Yordam Kitap.

———. 2015. *Ekonomide Hızlı Büyüme ve Balon*. Translated by B. Akalın. İstanbul: İletişim Yayınları.

Brown, E.H. 2007. *Web of Debt: The Shocking Truth about Our Money System*. Baton Rouge: Third Millennium Press.

Buğra, A. 1994. *State and Business in Modern Turkey: A Comparative Study*. New York: State University of New York Press.

Burton, M.G., and J. Higley. 1987. Elite Settlements. *American Sociological Review* 52 (3): 295–307.

———. 2001. The Study of Political Elite Transformations. *International Review of Sociology* 11(2): 181–199.

Castells, M. 2009. *The Rise of the Network Society: The Information Age: Economy, Society, and Culture*. Vol. 1. Oxford: Wiley Blackwell.

Chang, H., and I. Grabel. 2005. *Kalkınma Yeniden: Alternatif İktisat Politikaları El Kitabı*. Translated by E. Özçelik. İstanbul: İmge Kitabevi.

Collier, Ruth Berins. 1999. *Paths Towards Democracy: The Working Class and Elites in Western Europe and South America*. Cambridge, UK: Cambridge University Press.

Crouch, C. 2016. *Post Demokrasi*. Ankara: Dost Kitabevi.

Curtis, N. 2015. *İdiotizm: Kapitalizm ve Hayatın Özelleştirilmesi*. Translated by M. Ratip. İstanbul: İletişim Yayınları.

Dahl, R.A. 2005. *Who Governs? Democracy and Power in an American City*. New Haven: Yale University Press.

Dahrendorf, R. 1962. Eine neue deutsche Oberschicht? Notizen über die Eliten der Bundesrepublik. *Die Neue Gesellschaft* 9: 18–31.

Freeman, A., and B. Kagartlitsky. 2007. *Küreselleşmenin Krizi*. Translated by İ. Yıldız and B. Kara. İstanbul: Yordam Kitap.

Friedman, M. [1962] 2002. *Capitalism and Freedom*. Fortieth Anniversary Edition. California: The University of Chicago Press.

Fukuyama, F. 1989. The End of History? *The National Interest* 16: 3–18.

Gouldner, A. 1979. *Future of Intellectuals and the Rise of a New Class*. New York: Seabury Press.

Gusterson, H. 2015. Elites, Anthropology of. In *International Encyclopedia Of The Social & Behavioral Sciences*, ed. James D. Wright, vol. 7, 386–390. Amsterdam: Elsevier.

Hartmann, M. 2015. Elites: Sociological Aspects. In *International Encyclopedia of The Social & Behavioral Sciences*, ed. James D. Wright, vol. 7, 396–402. Amsterdam: Elsevier.

Harvey, D. 2007. *A Brief History of Neoliberalism*. Oxford: Oxford University Press.

———. 2008. *Yeni Emperyalizm*. Translated by H. Güldü. İstanbul: Everest Yayınları.

———. 2014. *Post Modernliğin Durumu*. Translated by S. Savran. İstanbul: Metis Yayınları.

———. 2015. *Neoliberalizmin Kısa Tarihi*. Translated by A. Onacak. İstanbul: Sel Yayıncılık.

Holcombe, R. 2016. *Politik Kapitalizm*. Translated by A. *Yayla*. *Liberal Düşünce Dergisi* 84: 103–125. https://dergipark.org.tr/en/pub/liberal/issue/48154/609216.

Hunter, F. 1953. *Community Power Structure: A Study of Decision Makers*. Chapel Hill: The University of North Carolina Press.

Iversen, T., and D. Soskice. 2019. *Democracy and Prosperity: Reinventing Capitalism through a Turbulent Century*. Princeton and Oxford: Princeton University Press.

Kahan, A.S. 1992. *Aristocratic Liberalism: The Social and Political Thought of Jacob Burckhardt, John Stuart Mill, and Alexis de TocquevilIe*. Oxford: Oxford University Press.

Keller, S. 1991. *Beyond the Ruling Class. Strategic Elites in Modern Society*. New Brunswick: Transaction Publications.

Keynes, J.M. [1936] 1973. *The General Theory of Employment Interest and Money*. London: Macmillan.

Kolko, G. 1963. *The Triumph of Conservatism: A Reinterpretation of American History, 1900–1916*. New York: The Free Press.

Korom, P. 2015. Elites: History of the Concept. In *International Encyclopedia Of The Social & Behavioral Sciences*, ed. James D. Wright, vol. 7, 390–395. Amsterdam: Elsevier.

Kurz, H.D. 2018. Power – The Bête Noire in Much of Modern Economics. *Artha Vijnana* LX (4): 319–376.

La Vere Bates, D. 1973. The Origins and Career Path Development of the Modern Turkish Business Elite. Unpublished doctoral dissertation, Department of Business Administration, University of Arkansas, pp. 59–60.

Mannheim, K. 1940. *Man and Society in the Age of Reconstruction*. New York: Harcourt, Brace.

Michels, R. 1999. *Political Parties: A Sociological Study of the Oligarchical Tendencies of Modern Democracy*. New Brunswick: Transaction Publications.

Milanovic, B. 2019. *Capitalism, Alone*. Cambridge, MA: Harvard University Press.

Mills, C. W. [1956] 2000. *The Power Elite*. USA: Oxford University Press.

Mosca, G. 1939. *The Ruling Class*. New York and London: McGraw-Hill Book Company.

O'Donnell, G.A., and P.C. Schmitter. 1986. *Transitions from Authoritarian Rule: Tentative Conclusions About Uncertain Democracies*. Washington, DC: Johns Hopkins University Press.

Ortega y Gasset, J. 1957. *The Revolt of the Masses*. New York: Norton.

Pakulski, J. 2012. The Weberian Foundations of Modern Elite Theory and Democratic Elitism. *Historical Social Research* 37 (1): 38–56.

Panitch, L., and S. Gindin. 2012. Kapitalizmde Krizler ve Bu Defaki Kriz. In *Bu Defaki Kriz*, ed. L. Panitch, G. Albo, and V. Chipper, 15–35. İstanbul: Yordam Kitap.

Pareto, V. 1916. *Trattato di sociologia generale*. Vol. 1. Firenze: G. Barbera.

———. 1935. *The Mind and Society*. Vol. III. London: Jonathan Cape.

Phillips, P. 2018. *Giants: The Global Power Elite*. New York: Seven Stories Press.

Piketty, T. 2014. *Capitalism in the Twenty-First Century*. Cambridge, MA: Belknap Press.

———. 2015. *Yirmi Birinci Yüzyılda Kapital*. Translated by H. Koçak. İstanbul: Türkiye İş Bankası Kültür Yayınları.

Polanyi, K. 2008. *Büyük Dönüşüm*. Translated by A. Buğra. İstanbul: İletişim Yayınları.

Pröbristing, M. 2011. Emperyalizm ve Kapitalizmin Çöküşü. In *Marksist Kriz Teorisi ve Kredi Krizi*, ed. R. Brenner and M. Pröbristing, pp. 61–112. Translated by S. Çakmak ve A. Şen Taşbaşı. İstanbul: Yordam Kitap.

Savran, S. 2013. *Üçüncü Büyük Depresyon*. İstanbul: Yordam Kitap.

Scheiring, G. 2020. *The Retreat of Liberal Democracy. Authoritarian Capitalism and the Accumulative State in Hungary*. Cham: Palgrave Macmillan.

Schumpeter, J. A. [1942] 2008. *Capitalism, Socialism and Democracy*. New York: First Harper Perennial Thought Edition.

Spash, C. L. 2017. *Routledge Handbook of Ecological Economics*. London and New York: Routledge.

Stigler, G.J. 1971. The Theory of Economic Regulation. *The Bell Journal of Economics and Management Science* 2: 3–21.

Stiglitz, J. 2011. Of the 1%, by the 1%, for the 1%. *Vanity Fair*, March 31.

Streeck, W. 2016. *Satın Alınan Zaman Demokratik Kapitalizmin Gecikmiş Krizi*. Translated by K. Kabadayı. İstanbul: Koç Üniversitesi Yayınları.

Svolik, M.W. 2009. Power Sharing and Leadership Dynamics in Authoritarian Regimes. *American Journal of Political Science* 53 (2): 477–494.

Türel, O. 2017. *Küresel Tarihçe: 1945–79*. İstanbul: Yordam Kitap.

Wahl, A. 2015. *Refah Devletinin Yükselişi ve Düşüşü*. Translated by H. Ünal ve B. Öztürk. İstanbul: h2o Kitap.

Wieser von, F. 1910. *Recht und Macht*. Leipzig: Duncker & Humblot.

———. 1926. *Das Gesetz der Macht*. Vienna: Julius Springer.

Wolfe, A. [1956] 2000. Afterword. In *The Power Elite*, C. W. Mills, [1956] 2000. Oxford: Oxford University Press.

Zuba, K. 2016. Power Holders: One Versus Many: Leadership and Elite Theories. *Journal of Political Power* 9 (2): 269–287.

CHAPTER 3

# Mill on Majority Power and Elite Government

**Abstract** J. S. Mill's (1806–1873) political participation and democracy approach was based on the philosophy of science that he introduced in *System of Logic* ([1843] 1973). Mill differentiated the "primary principles" and "secondary principles". Primary principles were the accepted laws of the field, based on historical scientific evolution. Secondary principles were the transformations of the primary principles when adopted for certain cases by the impact of "disturbing causes". The Millian narrative about the best form of government was also under the influence of his moral philosophy. Mill proposed secondary principles to lighten the weight of the principle of utility. He based his utilitarian philosophy on a different causality when compared to that of Bentham, arguing that secondary principles were discovered by induction. A. de Tocqueville's (1805–1859) method was significant since it was consistent with the causality approach on which Millian philosophy of science was based. Consistent with this approach, Tocqueville did not confine himself to the current political laws but also discussed the empirical spatial, temporal, and environmental laws during the development of the phenomenon or the case he discussed.

**Keywords** Philosophy of science • Moral philosophy • Method • Causality • Primary principles • Secondary principles • Bentham • Tocqueville



G. Baş Dinar, Ç. Akdere, *Tensions Between Capitalism and Democracy Today From the Perspective of J. S. Mill and J. A. Schumpeter*, https://doi.org/10.1007/978-3-031-45547-6_3

P. Smart stated his paper with the following phrase: "Mill was an elitist." Why? Smart characterized the national tone of Millian policy as elitist. His justification was based on "his advocacy for a distinct form of meritocratic representative government and his 'perfectionist' ontology, incorporating a qualitative hierarchical order of traits, which informed directly his analysis of nationalism and national self-determination" (Smart 1992, 527). However, M. Zouboulakis' (2005) study did not cite nationalism but the guarantor of individual self-development policy with conflict-less, quasi egalitarianist, participatory, and representative political and economic institutions. Then, it was Baum's turn (1999, 524), for him the ultimate goal is to extend democratic self-government, on equal terms, to virtually all working people with respect to their economic enterprises, within a competitive market economy: "ultimate goal is to extend democratic self-government, on equal terms, to virtually all working people with respect to their economic enterprises, within a competitive market economy." J. S. Mill's (1806–1873) political objective was to balance political power to promote the public interest. In other words, individual rights should be protected while maximizing public happiness in the future stationary society. How could this aim be achieved? To answer that question, we need to establish how Mill associated capitalism and democracy.

Where could Millian democracy fit within similar or conflicting theories such as liberal democracy, classical pluralism, participatory democracy, and competitive democracy (Cunningham 2002 cited by Bilir and Şahin 2021)? When compared to the two extremes, namely, J.-J. Rousseau's (1712–1778) (2002, 201) democracy that emphasized participation and equality and J. A. Schumpeter's (1883–1950) school of the "realist democracy theory", Mill is somewhere in the middle. Mill, like Rousseau, did not reject the common will that emerged with participation, and he was not afraid to confront undemocratic but "expedient" efforts such as Schumpeter. However, it could be suggested that his point on the above-mentioned scale was closer to Schumpeter since Rousseau did not precisely equate democracy with a certain economic order (Bilir and Şahin 2021). Classical pluralists such as Mill and Schumpeter were close to democracy since both "conflict" and competition were important in both.

The conflict between the masses and the elites could also be observed in the Millian narrative. As indicated by Barker (2015), Mill, in *Considerations on Representative Government* ([1861a] 1977), rejected secret ballots and electoral pledges and advocated a constitutional council and graduate enfranchisement. Thus, Mill could defend undemocratic practices by contrasting two issues: the legitimacy and competence of the rulers. Barker's (2015, 1) view was as follows: "The continual readjustment between the power of the masses and that of the elites was the methodology in Mill's *Considerations on Representative*."

Furthermore, the influence of the elites on the decisions of the representative government was not unproblematic. There was conflict between these parties. If we had to respond to this question based on Millian texts, we should first search for the influence of the elites on ruling elites in the Millian narrative because the conflicts between ruling elites would reflect the conflicts between the interests of other elites who influenced them.

For Mill, the bridge between democracy and capitalism was liberalism. Mill defended classical liberalism based on freedom of expression and speech, personal autonomy, and pluralism (Ward 2022). He argued that bureaucratic governments without these foundations would exercise the "despotism of custom" on individual freedoms. His example was China in the nineteenth century. According to Mill, the "despotism of custom" affected capital accumulation and human improvement (Xiao 2021).

Why is there debate on whether Mill was libertarian or authoritarian? According to Kurer, this was because "Mill's rules of government intervention were usually ambiguous". According to him, "This left little room for government intervention, and Mill was an unyielding defender of individual liberties against the encroachment of the state" (Kurer 1989, 457).

Mill asked the following question: What is the best form of representative government? He concluded that, "Ideally, the best form of government is representative government" (Mill ([1861a] 1977). The 'best' in this question actually meant the most suitable form of government for the accumulation of wealth. He provided a quite vague response: "Ideally, the best form of government does not mean the practicable or eligible one in all states of civilization but the practicable and eligible one under circumstances, achieved with the greatest amount of immediate and prospective benefits" (Mill ([1861a] 1977).

Mill has been accepted as one of the philosophers who predominantly contributed to the idea of democracy by advocating the need for public participation in government and as a "political elitist" for emphasizing competent leadership in government (Thompson 1976 cited by Warner 2001). According to Warner (2001), the reason for this confusion was his emphasis on "citizens". However, it should not be ignored that he introduced a synthesis of "public participation" and "competent leadership". An interesting literature that included the oeuvres of those who understood Mill has emerged. Thus, "the discussion that grew out of this literature included schemes for a more democratic public administration or to establish the legitimacy of a seemingly undemocratic institution within a political system that assumed democratic objectives" (Warner 2001, 404).

According to Urbinati, Mill's contribution to the modern theory of democracy could be understood by looking at ancient Greece. Mill sought to assign a deliberative and argumentative character to modern representative government based on the Republic of Athens (Green 2019). According to Urbinati (2006), Mill's theoretical work on democracy was built on three pillars: (1) the deliberative form of politics, (2) the authority of individual judgement and a cooperative policy model, and (3) family and economic relations. Furthermore, Mill argued that there were two heroes in a government: legislative institutions, namely, the Parliament (and legislative committees), and the executive branch and the larger public that included individuals, the media, civil associations, and political movements. Certain institutions are in conflict in this structure, namely, proportional representation, plural voting, and public voting. Mill believed that the first two were necessary to improve the audibility of 'minority voices' in public deliberations. According to Urbinati, the success of the former was more likely than the latter.

We have mentioned that the first issue in the Millian narrative about the best form of government was the influence of his moral philosophy. The second philosophical dimension was the influence of the philosophy of science. This was evident in the phrase "We have now examined the three fundamental conditions of the adaptation of the forms of government to the people who would be governed by these" (Mill ([1861a] 1977, 378) and in the book in general. According to Millian philosophy of science, the conditions should be considered during the implementation of the form of government that he determined within his theoretical framework. Here, the conflict between the "general causes" and "disturbing causes" was presented with the inverse deductive method. This form should be adapted to the relevant country after the determination of the "general causes" discussed in the theoretical framework. In this process, the "disturbing causes", namely, historical and institutional facts about the country would be employed.

Mill's only contribution was the assignment of individual incentives at the center of moral and political philosophy and economic theory. Mill's methodological individualism explained all social phenomena by the "reconstruction of individuals' motivations associated with the related phenomenon and the description of the phenomenon by the sum of individual behaviors dictated by these motivations" (Boudon 1985, 644, cited by Mouchot 2003, 214).

Mill's methodological individualism adhered to two causal principles, which are for Mill's fundamental distinction in the natural order. They are described in Book III of the *System of Logic* (1848). We call them the principle of the composition of causes (PCC) and the principle of heteropathic causality (PHC). The PCC represented "the case where the effect that combined causes is the sum of their separate effects", and the laws of this case corresponded to those "that operate together without alteration" (Mill [1843] 1973, 373–374). For the PHC, it applied to cases where "the combined effect of the causes is heterogeneous with respect to the sum of their separate effects" (Mill [1843] 1973, 373–374) and the laws of the second case reflected those "that cease to operate together" (Mill [1843] 1973, 373–374 cited by Akdere 2021). Millian analysis shared the following argument by Marshall: "economics cannot be compared to the exact physical sciences; for it deals with the ever-changing and subtle forces of human nature" (Marshall [1890] 1920, 14).

Fagot-Largeault affirmed (2002, 943) that Mill "argued in second case [the case of causal heteropathy] that the effects were heterogeneous with respect to their causes, and [for that reason] Mill called the natural regularities rebellious to the law of composition as 'heteropathic laws'. These were Mill's 'heteropathic effects', effects other than the simple 'sum' of effects of their combined cause that G.H. Lewes (1879) called 'emergents' effects". Mill's economic epistemology stated that "to judge how one will act under various desires and aversions which concurrently operate upon one must know how one would act under the exclusive influence of each one in particular" (Mill [1836a] 2003, 322). Here, Mill provided separate analyses for the effects of "aversion to labor, and desire of the present joy of expensive indulgences" (Mill [1836a] 2003, 322; Mill [1843] 1973, 902), two obstacles to the desire for wealth. The fact that Mill emphasized these obstacles demonstrated that he not only considered the pursuit of self-interest a behavioral motive but also indicated the dominance of psychological factors, customs, and habits on human behavior.

## Political Science Shaped by the Philosophy of Science

Mill's political participation and democracy approach was based on the philosophy of science that he introduced in *System of Logic* ([1843] 1973) (Akdere 2021). In particular, it was based on the causality introduced in the third chapter of the book. According to this approach, it would not be accurate to explain a specific event based only on the general laws achieved by deduction because that would only reveal the "general causes" behind the event. However, behind each event lie various historical and institutional factors. A close examination of these events would demonstrate that the "general causes" are only some of the factors that affect the event. In fact, there are several causes that lead to an event and deteriorate, increase or decrease the impact of "general causes". Mill called these "disturbing causes". Starting out with laws of deduction, the researcher should then focus on spatial, temporal, and environmental effects on the phenomenon or event. This focus is an inductive process in research. Mill called this the "specific experiment" in his study on social and economic facts and events. In a postdeductive inductive "specific experiment", the researcher attempts to determine and recognize "disturbing causes" that contradict or affect the "general causes".

Mill was not alone in the application of this scientific approach, which was also called the "reverse deductive" or "historical method" in *System of Logic* Book VI. Mill argued that the same research methodology was utilized and appreciated the most by the French political philosopher and pioneer sociologist Alexis de Tocqueville (1805–1859). This idea was discussed in several Mill essays, including *De Tocqueville on Democracy in America I*, *De Tocqueville on Democracy in America II*, and *State of Society in America* published in 1835, 1840, and 1836b, respectively.

The distance between Mill and deduction was based on the inadequacy of the method when applied to social events. What we put on the glasses of Mill's philosophy of science, we could see that reverse engineering could not be applied to social events, similar to certain natural events. For example, reverse engineering is useless in understanding the factors behind a chemical composition. Although a chemical composite can be subjected to various processes, the elements cannot be separated into the causes or elements that form the composite. We know that oxygen and hydrogen can form water. However, neither any process nor the laws of oxygen and hydrogen deductively could argue that when these two come together, they must form water (Mill [1843] 1973, 440).

As demonstrated by Mill's adoption of the abovementioned scientific research method, he was never a strict practitioner of deductive scientific principles or rules. This is the main element that distinguished him from Bentham. In "On the Definition of Political Economy; and on the Method of Investigation Proper to it" ([1836a] 2003) and collected essays in the book *Utilitarianism* ([1861b] 1969), Mill differentiated the "primary principles" and "secondary principles". Primary principles were the accepted laws of the field, based on historical scientific evolution. Secondary principles were the transformations of the primary principles when adopted for certain cases by the impact of "disturbing causes". In other words, Mill wanted scientists not to be blind practitioners of the primary principles determined by the discipline. Thus, he adapted the primary principles he inherited from Bentham based on historical and spatial conditions. In his analysis, he consulted knowledge on other fields. Through this transformation, he derived the secondary principles.

In his analysis of the economic and political structure of a society, Mill employed the abovementioned philosophy of science and methodology. Thus, he did not forget that the laws that governed the capitalist system explained the dynamics of British society at a certain time. Such specific laws cannot be expected to explain the dynamics of every society. Political economy, which determines the basic means of production and distribution, should in certain cases utilize the findings of other disciplines. Even when these findings invalidated his findings, new data should be analyzed. Based on this methodology, the fact that democratic characteristics could vary between societies should be considered. Mill's views on the relationship between democracy and capitalism are analyzed based on the abovementioned information.

The scientific character of the analysis was based on the hierarchy between the levels of laws. According to Mill, political economy, politics and history were separate branches of social sciences, the deductive approach that aimed to analyze "the acts of collective masses, and various phenomena that constitute social life" (Mill [1843] 1973, 875). The hierarchy of laws had three levels: higher-level laws, lower-level laws and the midway laws of human traits. The first group included complex laws of social sciences, lower-level laws were about the nature of individuals, and midway laws were about human traits; in other words, these were the subject matter of ethology. Thus, the economic phenomena were "the result of the composition of psychological and ethological laws" (Mill [1843] 1973, 896) (Zouboulakis 2005).

## Individual Interest Versus Collective Interest

Indeed, according to Mill, the objective of economic policies was not the "geometric man" but the "man in a state of society" because for him, capitalist relations are conducted in a "state of society". Policy makers should take this into account. Millian political philosophy, fueled by utilitarianism, argued that when a policy is "expedient", individual liberties could be restricted and a government intervention could be implemented. This could happen due to freedom, security, equality, diversity, and eradication of poverty: "If government intervention could lead to an overall 'progress' (in Mill, it is associated with increased happiness), then government intervention is justified. Furthermore, constitution should be consistent with the ideals and assure the implementation of 'progressive' policies" (Kurer 1989, 480).

Millian corpus in all fields could be summarized by the following two sentences by F. Thilly (1923, 1): "Although Mill's fame as a philosopher rested largely upon his work as a logician, his chief interest was the application of principles to practical affairs" and "he was driven by the desire to discover a rational foundation for human conduct and institutions" Mill suggested that all social phenomena could be explained by psychological and ethological laws (Thilly 1923, 5).

G. Varouxakis (2002) cited *Considerations on Representative Government Mill* ([1861a] 1977, 548) to describe the association between nationality and liberal values: it is in general a necessary condition of free institutions, that the boundaries of governments should coincide in the main with those of nationalities." It could be argued that there was a link between Millian liberalism and the concept of national character because Mill emphasized character; he even introduced an ethological science that focused on this issue. He considered it an alternative to phrenology (Leary 1982). His two books on liberalism, *Considerations on Representative Government Mill* ([1861a] 1977) and *On Liberty*, published two years later, argued that members of the modern democratic society should also be trained in "civic character". He considered personality and civic character as two sides of a coin. He also argued that the regime—according to him, there were two types of regimes—despotic and democratic—affected the character of the individual. There were also two types of characters: "active" and "passive". He argued that "active characters" were more compatible with democratic regimes since they engage in political activities (Ball 2000).

Mill believed that to be a liberal did not required the denial of the superiority of certain natures, or the claim to rule based on some superior worth (axios)" (Barker, 2015, 1). This, which could be summarized as accepting "the rule of the wise for the wise", was a progress according to Mill. "Professional politicians" would create the best order, namely, "*eunomia*". Thus, it could be suggested that Mill was again under the influence of Tocqueville. "Professional politicians" would also improve participation and competence.

The idea of progress was associated with the idea of the improvement of individual potential in Mill. The idea of justice was also associated with the idea of justice for the masses. These ideas, which constituted the British philosopher's utilitarian philosophy, emphasized that progress and justice were the outcomes of a historical process (Persky 2016). Competition between political leaders could be hampered by the hereditary privileges of certain leaders.

For individuals to know and recognize their own interests, they should possess certain traits. Prominent traits include psychological health and criminal liability. These two factors are required for the perception of self-interest. The interests of individuals without these traits are managed by their parents or attorneys. Additionally, individuals are members of certain social classes or nations. An individual's "self-benefit" could also be measured by its consistency with the general interests of the groups to which the individual belongs. Acceptance of this means that these groups are also aware of their interests and take care of these interests. What should be done when individuals or groups do not know their benefits or cannot act to protect them? Several philosophers have attempted to answer this question, including T. Hobbes (1588–1679), J. Bentham (1748–1832), J. Mill (1773–1836), J. S. Mill and Tocqueville. They all agreed that such a situation would require the intervention of an authority to protect the interests of these individuals and groups. In other words, authority should defend the "collective interests". To understand this concept, the concepts of "individual interest" and "collective interest", introduced by Mill, should be clarified.

To understand Mill's approach to democracy and elites, we should initially focus on the legitimacy of power as an individual interest and collective interest. To be able to do that, the definitions of "individual interest" and "collective interest" needed.

Several philosophers, including Hobbes, Bentham, Mill, and Tocqueville, described power as an authority that should step in and protect the interests of individuals and groups. In other words, power should look after the "collective interest". Mill also proposed the measurement of "individual interest" based on conformity to the general interests of the groups associated with the individual. This further required the awareness and protection of their self-interests by these groups. According to Mill, power must nurture the "collective interest".

Mill was interested in the concept of "collective interest" based on both the philosophy of utilitarianism and liberalism and questioned the role of authority in a liberal economy. Thus, capitalism, which was based on basic freedoms such as the freedom of property and investment, was directly affected by the decisions of the authority on these issues. As Mill questioned the concept of "collective interest", he criticized Hobbes and Bentham for oversimplifying the concept of "interest of the rulers"; on the other hand, he approached the philosophy of Tocqueville. Mill questioned the legitimacy and founding ideas of the ruling class. According to Mill, several "communes" (fins communes) could be pursued by rulers. For example, according to Hobbes, there could only be a single unifying purpose: fear. In Hobbes' world, the "state of society" is the fear of the people (Mill [1843] 1973, 889).

The interaction between Mill and Tocqueville was based on the idea of a "social situation" called democracy, attributed to the United States, France, and other modern societies. The democracy approach that emerged with the analysis of these two nations also provides information about governmental movements. However, to understand democracy, a closer look is necessary at the definition of the "social situation" as proposed by Mill.

To clarify, Mill attempted to decompose the factors that led to democracy as a "social condition". He did this by trying to understand how interests should be pursued in a democratic order. According to Mill, there are two types of interests: the interest of the governor and the interest of the governed. Mill ([1843] 1973, 891) inferred that first (1) general behavior of the rulers was only determined by their interests; second, (2) a complete consistency with the interests of the governed could only be achieved by taking responsibility. To describe the differences between these two dimensions of the interest of the governor, a deeper look is required at Mill's moral philosophy that was developed based on Bentham's moral philosophy. The description of "majority power", which is the difference between Millian and Benthamian utilitarianism, could be of great assistance. Thus, we should focus on how Mill tried to replace Bentham's "majority power" concept.

## Bentham and the Highest Interest of Majority

Bentham's position and his attitude towards the acts of the ruling class were quite different when compared to Hobbes. Bentham considered the attitudes of rulers (i.e., subsequent kings or an entire body, a majority, a nation, an aristocracy, or a representative assembly). According to him, the acts of the majority become the acts of the entire body (Mill, [1843] 1973, 890), which leads to the question "how are the acts of the entire body?"

Mill's utilitarianism is developed based on Bentham's "principle of utility," which Bentham defined and discussed in his book *An Introduction to the Principles of Morals and Legislation* ([1789] 1970). Mill's approach was first mentioned in his essay "On Bentham" ([1838] 1998). Later, the essay "Utilitarianism" was published in Fraser's Magazine in 1861 as a three-article series. This essay was first published as a book in 1863. Due to these two texts, Mill, along with his father Mill and the English philosopher Bentham, became one of the three prominent utilitarian philosophers.

The principle of utility was based on an approach called the calculation of pleasure (*felicific calculus*) or "calculation of utility" by Mill. The first chapter of the book, "Of the Principle of Utility", described this principle. According to the principle, a degree or amount of calculable pleasure could be induced by a particular behavior. The "calculus of pleasure" (*felicific calculus*), according to Bentham, entailed any parameter that could be utilized to calculate happiness: the intensity of pleasure and pain (their strength), their duration, the certainty or uncertainty of their occurrence, their proximity or distance (whether they will happen soon or after a long time), their fertility (the probability of subsequent similar sensations), their purity (the probability of subsequent contrasting sensations), and their scope (the number of individuals they affect) (Bentham, [1789] 1970; Mitchell, 1918).

Economists benefited the most from the legacy of utilitarian philosophy. The efforts of the English economist W. S. Jevons (1835–1882) to quantify "utility", a qualitative concept, was the most significant development that altered the course of the history of economic philosophy. Inspired by the *felicific calculus* that entailed the subtraction of the amount of individual pleasure from the amount of pain, Jevons based the concept of "economic utility" on this calculation in the 1870s. As N. Sigot (2001, 22) indicated, pleasure and pain are our primary sensations that underlie happiness according to Bentham. Furthermore, they are the only drivers of all human behavior. Behaviors that lead to more pleasure than pain were considered "economically beneficial". Although individual and then social *felicific calculus* was first discussed by Bentham, Jevons' work was limited to the individual dimension. After the 1960s, economists who contributed to Welfare Economics, notably V. Pareto (1848–1923) and A. Pigou (1877–1959), extended the calculus to the social dimension. Nevertheless, it should be noted that the legacy of utilitarianism has been embraced not only by economics but also by several fields from political science to psychology and from sociology to educational sciences.

James Mill referred to his son's education as "a lesson on Benthamite theory" in "Education" ([1824] 1992) (See Sigot 1995, 275–276). Based on this utilitarian practice, a closer look is required at utilitarianism to understand Mill's education. As mentioned in his autobiography (Mill [1873] 1993, 79), reading *An Introduction to the Principles of Morals and Legislation* (1789), Bentham's magnum opus, in his early youth was a cornerstone in his life and promoted his intellectual development. He wrote that when he finished the last chapter, he became a completely different individual. He disclosed that the "principle of utility" he encountered in the book became the keystone on which he built his knowledge and beliefs and which facilitated his integral understanding of several topics. After the discovery of this principle, he wrote, "I now had opinions; a creed, a doctrine, a philosophy; in one (and the best) sense of the word, a religion" (Mill [1873] 1993, 68). Instilling and spreading this religion became the most important goal in his life, and he thought he could change the world with this doctrine (Mill [1873] 1981, 68).

The "principle of utility", the first pillar of Benthamian philosophy, means "the greatest happiness of the highest number" (Roquet 1889, XVII–XVIII). It aims to "to make the individual, as much as possible, a means of happiness first for herself and then for other beings" (Sigot 1995, 272 cited by Mill 1824, 139). Thus, reform is necessary, and Benthamian utilitarianism was one of the core philosophical concepts. However, since Bentham criticized the concept of reform in his autobiography, it would be fair to argue that Mill became the reformer he wanted to be, not what his father wanted him to be. For him, being a reformer was a role that could only be assigned to two individuals: the artist and the scientist. The artist determines and defines the purpose, while the scientist searches for the desired effect, determines the possibilities, experiences them and makes others experience them as well. In the end, it is the artist who practices the approved possibilities (Robson 1989, 22).

According to Bentham ([1789] 1970, 173–174), everyone calculates, "Men calculate, some with less exactness, indeed, some with more: but all men calculate". According to him, the only underlying reason for human behavior is sensations, and they are so continuous that they become scientific or artistic objects (Bentham 1785–6, 30419 cited by Sigot 2001). Thus, Bentham revealed the objective dimension of his philosophy. Individual utility is based on individual pleasures and pain, namely, personal interests. Bentham's famous sentence sums up exactly the very idea: "Nature has placed mankind under the governance of two sovereign masters, pain and pleasure. [...] They govern us in all we do, in all we say, in all we think" (Bentham [1789] 1970, 11).

The Benthamian philosophy of utilitarianism, which identified the above-mentioned routine, explored the iteration and predictability of human behavior. The "principle of utility" is a scientific principle that could help us do just that. Benthamism was accepted as a type of 'moral Newtonianism' because utilitarian philosophy and Newtonian physics were analogous (Halevy 1901–1904, 289–290; Cot 1992; Touchard [1958] 1985). The "principle of utility" is to Benthamian utilitarianism what gravity is to Newtonian physics. While Newtonian physics always explains natural phenomena with gravity, Benthamian utilitarianism always explains human behavior and social phenomena with the "principle of utility".

It has, however, been questioned whether the empirical foundation of utilitarian philosophy was sufficient to call it scientific. According to C. Audard (1998, 5), Benthamite marginalist economists discussed hedonist and associative psychology on the one hand and moral neutralization trends on the other, demonstrating that the explanation of human behavior was based on various interpretations of utilitarian legacy.

According to Mill, the explanation of human behavior with a single principle would be a reductionist approach, which was not adequate for the complex nature of behavior. Although he adopted the analogy established by Benthamian utilitarianism with Newtonian physics, he did not hesitate to question it. As argued by Sigot (2001, 17), the principle of utility could explain all behavior according to Bentham. All behavior that does not fit the principle could always be attributed to ignorance or stupidity: a criminal is just a poorly informed calculator if the laws are robust. The decisive step is taken when Bentham declares that the principle of utility is this universal reference, spontaneously adopted, even unconsciously, by all individuals, "however stupid and perverse they may be" (Bentham [1789] 1970, 13), including understood by its most virulent detractors. Bentham excluded behavior that was not driven by pleasure or pain from his research. According to Sigot, when there are factors that confuse the individual and preclude self-interest, these were not associated with Bentham's analysis. More precisely, Bentham was so convinced about the objectivity of the "calculation of pleasure" that he was never worried about other possible acts of the individual. According to Bentham, it was the duty of the "deontologist" to explain their interests to those who did not know their interests because if people knew their interests, they could act based on these interests.

Mill's utilitarianism precisely opposed the abovementioned ideas. Mill described this opposition down to the last detail in "On Bentham" ([1838] 1998) that he wrote before *Utilitarianism*. While the Millian utilitarian philosophy did not examine individual or collective happiness, it still employed *felicific calculus*. Millian utilitarianism intervened when the Benthamite principle of utility failed to explain facts or cases. Thus, Millian utilitarianism did not establish what is "useful" and "just" interest but rather served "for weighing these conflicting utilities against one another, and marking out the region within which one or the other preponderates" (Mill ([1861b] 1969), 223).

People morally judge the events in their lives, while societies ensure happiness by enacting the most beneficial laws. In utilitarianism, "the greatest happiness of the majority" means general happiness. Although this definition seems fertile, it has been criticized for ignoring the happiness of minorities. Mill knew that these issues were not as simple as Bentham formulated; thus, he did not reduce human behavior to a quantification of pain and pleasure. He did not emphasize the "principle of utility" like Benthamian utilitarianism. He wrote that in certain cases, various types of benefits compete, and the moral behavior of individuals cannot be predicted in such cases. He insisted that a hierarchy of benefits should be established to rank these benefits.

Mill proposed secondary principles to lighten the weight of the principle of utility. He based his utilitarian philosophy on a different causality when compared to that of Bentham, arguing that secondary principles were discovered by induction. According to Mill, human behavior is multidimensional, and to understand it, the focus should be on the morality (rightness and wrongness of behavior), aesthetics (beauty of behavior), and sympathy (irresistibility of behavior) of the behavior (Wilson 1990,

83). This multidimensionality could be explored as follows: "actions are right in proportion as they tend to promote happiness, wrong as they tend to produce the reverse of happiness. By happiness is intended pleasure, and the absence of pain [...] To give a clear view of the moral standard set up by the theory, much more requires to be said; in particular, what things it includes in the ideas of pain and pleasure; and to what extent this is left an open question." (Mill ([1861b] 1969), 210).

The methodological meaning of this discourse can be summarized by the following words by Mill. The background of Bentham's utilitarian doctrine is fed by the following ideas: the movement is the result of a single force, not the clash of several forces, and every social phenomenon arises from the action of a single force, from a single feature of human nature (Mill ([1843] 1973), 888). Mill's utilitarianism, on the other hand, did not tout a "single power" or "a single human trait". Thus, Mill developed the doctrine of complex phenomena. Therefore, his utilitarianism was most open to change. He suggested that even behind the desire for things, there was a more complex motive structure apart from the Benthamite calculation of pleasure and pain.

The inclusion of the discussion in the *System of Logic* ([1843] 1973) made it clear that these issues were beyond the realm of utilitarianism but of science. It was also mentioned that the motive behind a behavior was not "always an expectation for pain or pleasure". This idea was revolutionary for the period. Thus, Mill added a reflection on diverse motives behind a behavior and the means by which they occur to Benthamian utilitarianism. However, Bentham remained true to his consequentialist approach to everything and was only concerned with the "purpose" or "outcome" of the behavior.

Mill distanced himself from the consequentialist approach since he believed that individual behavior was not quite outcome-oriented. Behind the behavior, he observed something such as "the action itself becomes an object of desire and is performed without reference to any motive beyond itself". According to Mill, the behavior became the "object of desire" beyond the pleasure and pain it caused. Under the influence of J. Mill's associationism, Millian utilitarianism focused on another idea: habitual actions independent of the pleasure that they could cause. He proposed harmful behaviors as an example. He argued that when we change a little, we consider these behaviors as not currently but potentially beneficial. He even argued that, "In this manner it is that habits of hurtful excess continue to be practised although they have ceased to be pleasurable" (Mill [1843] 1973, 842).

One of the reasons why these ideas were ahead of their time was that they were based on the unconscious later explored by S. Freud (1856–1939) and future expectations that were described in economics by J. M. Keynes (1883–1946). Mill mentioned that the individual acts only habitually, without calculating the potential pleasure and pain. Then, is this not an individual choice? This question has been answered with different responses in human history, but the one provided by Freud was the most resounding: we make a choice when we make calculations or act out of habit, but this choice is not conscious but based on the calculations and habits of the unconscious. American economist T. Veblen (1857–1929) suggests accepting individuals as "curious beings" rather than "fast calculators".

Urbinati argued that the Millian conception of freedom should be understood as freedom from arbitrary interference or "domination". Mill "believed in 'progressive beings'". He also assigned a task to the state to realize this: "he did believe that the state could train individuals to achieve this themselves." "First, the complexity of national and international public policies meant that only a professional administrative elite could make the relevant decisions efficiently—hence, he stressed the importance of civil service in the construction of integrated legislative programs."

This could also be explained with an example. Mill's last move was to measure the potential of the principle to explain a situation to stand firm against the "principle of utility" and to determine the bond he established with the principle more accurately. He found a concrete case and pondered how the principle worked in that case. He mentioned this several times in his book *Utilitarianism*, and he devoted most of the fifth chapter to this discussion. In fact, in the first chapter, he already prepared the reader by mentioning various approaches by different schools:

> for the philosophic supporters of that theory are now agreed that the intuitive perception is of principles of morality, and not of the details [...] If so, the intuitive ethics would coincide with the utilitarian, and there would be no further quarrel between them. Even as it is, the intuitive moralists, although they believe that there are other intuitive moral obligations, do already believe this to be one; for they unanimously hold that a large portion of morality turns upon the consideration due to the interests of our fellow creatures. Therefore, if the belief in the transcendental origin of moral obli-

gation gives any additional efficacy to the internal sanction, it appears to me that the utilitarian principle has already the benefit of it. (Mill [1861b] 1969, 230)

Every time a principle is used to explain a situation, it conflicts with a second principle. For example, an individual may prefer "imperfect happiness" as opposed to the principle of utility. That is, "happiness" and "satisfaction" are different. The kind of happiness we desire is questioned. According to Mill, the utilitarian individual is the one who knows how to endure imperfect happiness.

Millian utilitarianism constructed a classification for the quality of pleasure. Physical and mental pleasure levels were categorized into different groups. He argued that "imperfect happiness" was experienced mostly by those who preferred the secondary principles to the principle of utility. Thus, he did not aim to judge those who preferred the primary principle, namely, the principle of utility, but to explain the behavior of those who did not nor had the opportunity to experience mental pleasures and that of those who distanced themselves from intellectual pleasures over time. According to him, intellectual pleasures were both more permanent and less costly. Due to the "desire to be virtuous" or "possession of higher human faculties", humans are not caught up by the call of bodily pleasures. The way to develop the ability to prioritize intellectual pleasures was through education. The following text demonstrates that Mill did not center life on the principle of utility:

> I never indeed varied in the conviction that happiness is the test of all rules of conduct, and the end of life. However, I now thought that this end was only to be attained by not making it the direct aim. Those only are happy (I thought) who have their attention fixed on something other than their own happiness: on the happiness of others, either individually or collectively; on the improvement of mankind, even on some art or pursuit followed not as a means but as an ideal end. Aiming thus at something else, they find happiness by the way. The enjoyments of life (such was now my theory) are sufficient to make life pleasant when they are taken en passant, without being made a principal object. Once they make them so, however, they are immediately felt to be insufficient. They will not bear a scrutinizing examination: ask yourself if you are happy, and you cease to be so. (Mill [1873] 1981, 145–146)

As mentioned above, Mill's critique of Bentham was based on a methodological distrust. In Chap. 6 of the *System of Logic*, he examined Bentham's moral philosophy based on the methodological perspective. Mill called Benthamian methodology the "geometrical method in politics" (Mill [1843] 1973, 889). According to Bentham, rulers determine a system of government compatible with the general interest. What Bentham advocated was the "pure democracy that represented the majority". Advocating the idea of the maximization of collective happiness, Bentham argued that social philosophy and society should aim the conditions that would allow the "highest happiness of the many". J. Mill's response was both close and distant: representative democracy could not be constructed by defending the interests of the majority but by exploring the limits of personal freedoms. In addition, this could only be conducted by "wise people". J. Mill and J. S. Mill advocated the "representative democracy of the wise" (Akdere 2021, 272). In his essay on Tocqueville, Mill clearly stated the essence of this elitist approach in politics: "the best government, (need it be said?) must be the government of the wisest, and these must always be a few" (Mill [1835] 1977, 72). To better understand Mill's distance from Bentham, his closeness to Tocqueville should be elaborated.

## Tocqueville as the Mirror of Mill

Mill distanced himself from Bentham and Hobbes but adopted a different approach towards Tocqueville. The most important common similarity between Mill and Tocqueville was their approach to liberalism. Their correspondence and conversations during their physical encounters demonstrated that they had similar ideas, especially on the status of freedom. P. Thierry (1994) emphasized that Mill's famous book *On Liberty* ([1859] 1977) was based on the essays *De Tocqueville on Democracy in America I* ([1835] 1977) and *De Tocqueville on Democracy in America II* ([1840] 1977), where Tocqueville discussed his theses.

Tocqueville mirrored Mill also because both criticized Benthamian discourse and questioned the hazards of the majority rule. The Benthamian principle of "the greatest happiness of the highest number" was not clear about the main idea that the ruling class should be built on. How should the majority act? When answering these questions, Tocqueville provided the key to understanding "collective interest" and "personal interest" and assisted Mill in determining where to stand on the fine line between "freedom" and "utility".

J. Mill's admiration for Tocqueville was associated with the methodology adopted by the American philosopher. Father Mill's criticism of Bentham and Hobbes also lied in the scientific research methods they employed (Akdere 2021, 267). Mill, who had a special interest in methodology and based his approach on every issue that he wrote about on the philosophy of science, claimed that the abovementioned philosophers employed a "geometric or abstract methodology" that he found objectionable. The drawback of this method, a product of a priori reasoning, was that it led to an "abstract universality of findings" (Thierry 1994, 11). According to Mill, the most disturbing aspect of this method was its a priori description of all situations and tendencies of human nature and the employment of these descriptions to reach political inferences (Thierry 1998, 157). In contrast, Mill employed empiricism, quoting the British politician T. B. Macaulay, and called his method "the purely empirical method of chemistry" that analyzes the efficacy of institutions based on causality (Thierry 1998, 157–158). According to him, Tocqueville's method was similar to Macaulay's. This method, the perspective of which included historical events, knowledge on the real passions of people who live in a democracy, and special forms of suppression and oppression, was adequate for the analysis of the influence of political institutions that affect the pleasures of the people (Thierry 1994, 12). This method was a source of inspiration for his approach to social sciences.

Mill argued that Tocqueville was not only result-oriented but also paid attention to the means that led to the result. According to him, Tocqueville's initial analytical research on a case was based on both the general laws of human nature and observations (Thierry 1994, 12). Thus, Tocqueville's method based on both deduction and induction was similar to the Millian philosophy of science methodology. Mill commended Tocqueville, arguing that he made a difference by discovering the laws of the human mind and assessing the validity of empirical inferences. What he meant was the "specific experiment" described above.

According to Mill, the significance of Tocqueville's work was the method he employed rather than the results (Mill [1835 and 1840] 1997). For Mill, Tocqueville was the first to analyze the factors behind democracy based on the art and science of government. This was quite innovative for their period. As Mill stated in his essay *De Tocqueville on Democracy in America*, he constructed "general laws" that reveal "general causes" on the laws of human nature. He investigated the United States, France, and other modern societies about the "disturbing laws" induced by "disturbing causes". Tocqueville followed the same path. Thus, according to Mill, the scientific results of Tocqueville were not fed by a single channel (Mill [1835 and 1840] 1994). More precisely, Mill also observed his own methodical approach, which was a mixture of deduction and induction, in Tocqueville.

Mill criticized Bentham for assigning disproportionate significance to the decisions of the majority. The philosopher was closer to Tocqueville, whose political stance he considered closer when compared to that of Bentham. He extended his debate he conducted under the influence of the French philosopher to include a discussion on the quality of the representative democracy of an enlightened government.

Mill read Tocqueville quite carefully; later, Tocqueville stated that Mill was the philosopher who understood him the best (Thierry 1994, 7). Influenced by his summary of the second chapter of *De la Démocratie en Amérique* (Mill [1835 and 1840] 1994). Tocqueville also argued that Mill perceived the morals and details that his ideas aimed at the most (Thierry 1994, 7). Mill also cited Tocqueville with similar praise. He stated that it was not Tocqueville's job to get carried away by the views that were available for him. Thus, Mill considered Tocqueville "the starting point for a new era in political science education" (Mill [1835 and 1840] 1994, 156). This new era was the renewal period of political epistemology.

P. Thierry (1994), who published Mill's essays on Tocqueville in French, argued that the relationship between Mill and Tocqueville was not adequately discussed in the literature. Few authors who investigated the convergence of the two philosophers published different ideas. A. S. Kahan (1992) discussed the concept of "aristocratic liberalism" while J. Hamburger, H. O. Pappé, Mme. Mueller, J. Lively, and J-C. Lamberti investigated this relationship in other contexts.

Tocqueville's analysis included various human conditions, the complexity of the causes of human acts, and the legal capacity to predict these effects (Thierry 1994, 13). Thus, Tocqueville's method was significant since it was consistent with the causality approach on which Millian philosophy of science was based. Consistent with this approach, Tocqueville did not confine himself to the current political laws but also discussed the empirical spatial, temporal, and environmental laws during the development of the phenomenon or the case he discussed.

Thierry (1994, 10) called the influence of the French philosopher on Mill the "Tocqueville eclipse", as mentioned in Mill's autobiography. The Tocqueville eclipse helped reduce Bentham's influence on Mill's philosophy. Thus, Mill began with an interest in 'nuanced' socialism, then distanced himself from pure democracy and approached the somewhat 'altered' version of democracy described in *Considerations on Representative Government* ([1861a] 1977). To reiterate and recap, reading Tocqueville's *De la démocratie en Amérique* ([1835 and 1840] 1994) changed Mill's beliefs about political philosophy because his mind was intellectually ready for this change (Thierry 1994, 10).

According to Mill, when current laws could not predict human behavior, this was due to the inferences achieved without spatial, temporal, and environmental analysis of the behavior. Thus, the inability to understand and predict the behavior of the rulers was due to these inferences. The nature of rulers' decisions could only be understood with the analysis of the space, time, and environment where these decisions were made. These analyses would lead to a complex causality, the impact of which could not be predicted by current. Mill wanted to save social sciences, including economics and political science, from this impasse. The analysis of American society, which Tocqueville investigated with the scientific method described by Mill, was a qualitative approach that did not fall into the abovementioned impasse.

Inspired by the Tocquevillian method that employed both deduction and induction, Mill believed that empirical inferences were key to discovering the laws of the human mind. Based on this framework, Mill argued that rulers' decisions and behaviors could only be understood by the analysis of the space, time, and environment where these decisions were made. Thus, the Millian stance was similar to that of Schumpeter, who argued that human nature could not be simplified and entailed a complex mechanism.

## Democracy as State of Society

The interaction between Mill and Tocqueville was observed around the "state of society" called democracy as attributed to the US, France and other modern societies. The concept of democracy that emerged based on the analysis of these two nations also provided information about the acts of the government. However, to understand democracy, a closer look is required at the definition of the notion of "state of society" by Mill.

"States of society" is one of the main Millian concepts and was observed in each book authored by Mill on economics, politics, philosophy of science, and moral philosophy. "States of society" was mentioned in the sixth volume of *System of Logic*, dedicated to the epistemology of the "science of human nature"; in the political economy where Mill distinguished the laws of the mind and the laws of matter. While the forces pushing the individual to act in the "state of society" were explained by the former, the physical forces that governed "things" were defined and analyzed using the second. (Akdere 2021).

Although "state of society" could seem like a casual phrase, Mill employed it as a scientific term. The "state of society" is an actual consequence of several factors. As mentioned above, based on the Millian philosophy of science, every natural and social event should be analyzed based on "general causes" and "disturbing causes" to perceive its complex structure. The job of the social scientist is to identify these intertwined causes. The complexity of the causes of the "state of society" was explained by Mill as follows: "What is called a state of society, is the simultaneous state of all the greater social facts or phenomena. Such are, the degree of knowledge, and of intellectual and moral culture, existing in the community, and in every class of it" (Mill [1843] 1973, 911). Mill provided a list of social facts that led to this state: "the state of industry, of wealth and its distribution; the habitual occupations of the community; their division into classes, and the relations of those classes to one another; the common beliefs which they entertain on all subjects most important to mankind, and the degree of assurance with which those beliefs are held; their tastes, and the character and degree of their aesthetics development; their form of government, and the more important of their laws and customs. The condition of all these things, and of many more which will readily suggest themselves, constitute the state of society or the state of civilization at any given time." (Mill [1843] 1973, 912). Thus, all of the above-listed factors that cause it should be investigated to analyze any state of society.

The "disturbing causes" should also be part of the policy of analysis. In other words, they should consider diverse circumstances that include the behavior of everyone, even that of the government. They act based on complex causes, resulting in the inability of the laws to predict any particular cause or effect. This complexity stemmed from the simultaneous effects of the general and disturbing causes to produce the "state of society".

The discussion was well situated in the political debate once we familiarized ourselves with its proximity to the ideas of Tocqueville. The "everything" was defined based on the "state of society" and "collective interest" in both Mill and Tocqueville. The laws of political economy were developed in a specific "state of society" in the U.K., and they might not explain the operation of another "state of society". The following passage by Mill summarizes this idea (Akdere 2021):

"State of society" mostly induced by "disturbing causes". However, what are the data behind "disturbing causes"? Millian response was vague: "The condition of all these causes, and several others that are the state of the corporation or the state of the civilization at a given time would offer themselves—similar to the mind" (Mill [1843] 1973, 71). It should be remembered that time and the country create certain "ways of life and ideas", which determine the culture, a notion "inherent in the reflection of social sciences" (Cuche 2004, 3; Akdere 2021). The coexistence of social phenomena or social statistical consensus means moving from one state of society to another. According to Mill, social sciences should investigate the causes of the consequent states of society to understand the laws of transition (Thierry 1994, 13):

> The laws of the phenomena of society are, and can be, nothing but the laws of the actions and passions of human beings united together in the social state. Men, however, in a state of society, are still men; their actions and passions are obedient to the laws of individual human nature. Men are not, when brought together, converted into another kind of substance, with different properties; as hydrogen and oxygen are different from water, or as hydrogen, oxygen, carbon, and azote, are different from nerves, muscles, and tendons. Human beings in society have no properties but those that are derived from, and may be resolved into, the laws of the nature of individual man. In social phenomena the Composition of Causes is the universal law. (Mill [1843] 1973, 879)

For Mill, "several common goals" and "common purposes" bring people together and create a particular state of society. However, according to Hobbes, only one factor was effective: "fear". For Hobbes, "government was based on fear. [...] Mutual fear alone united men in the state of society" (Mill [1843] 1973, 889). To argue that "social contract" was based on fear, according to Mill, was a maxim of a first principle or a "petition of principle": "there is *petitio principii* here, since [...] any rule of conduct, even when it is as obligatory as could be accomplished with one promise, should itself be based on the theory of the subject" (Mill [1843] 1973, 889). However, "[i]t is true that Hobbes did not judge this maxim alone sufficient to carry all its conclusions" (Mill [1843] 1973, 889), and "the theory, therefore, cannot rely on it" (Mill [1843] 1973, 889). However,

Mill retained the same position: one cannot "take a practical principle, a precept as the basis of a theory." (Mill [1843] 1973, 889) (Akdere, 2021).

In his letter to Tocqueville dated October 3, 1835, Mill described the aim of the democrats. He mentioned that they wanted the people to elect the people who would govern them best rather than to find the means of government. He even argued that democrats provided these individuals as much space as possible to govern all tendencies. Mill criticized the French philosopher at this point. He emphasized that the dominance of the "public opinion" could begin to turn into despotism of the majority over time. Tocqueville, who did not usually respond to these criticisms, responded to those of Mill (Thierry 1994, 15–6).

Mill attempted to separate the factors of democracy, which is a "state of society" to clarify this. He tries to understand how interests are pursued in the democratic order. According to Mill, there were two types of interests: the interest of the governed and the interest of the rulers. Thus (Mill [1843] 1973, 891),

1. The average behavior of the rulers was determined only by self-interest.
2. A sense of consistency with the interests of the governed could only be produced by taking responsibility.

For the alignment between the interests of the rulers and the ruled, the principal interest of the rulers should be consistent with the principal interest of the ruled, leading to two further interest categories: "the interest of the ruler"" and "the interest of the governed" (Mill [1843] 1973, 890). They are connected to each other: "No rulers have their selfish interest identical with that of the governed, unless it be rendered so by accountability, that is, by dependence on the will of the governed" (Mill [1843] 1973, 890). In other words, "The principal interest of the rulers was "the desire of retaining or the fear of losing their power, " (Mill [1843] 1973, 890). Mill argued that the rule of the majority was based on the personal interests of the rulers, adding a third item to the above-listed two:

1. Self-interest of the rulers (maintaining power)
2. The interest of those who voted for the rulers
3. The interest of those who did not vote for the rulers

The political market includes politicians (who focus on job security, re-election, fundraising, popularity—their decisions affect their eligibility), bureaucrats, interest groups and voters. They collectively decide on the construction of a new highway, for example. However, self-interest and individual incentives also influence the political process and are the basis of political decisions.

Public choice theory in economics was dedicated to the investigation of politics through an economic lens. The public choice theory argued that, like everyone else, those who govern, who were supposed to focus on "public interest", also focus on personal interest, well-being and preferences, money, love, family and security. They could be conflicted in concerns such as money, love, family, and security in their efforts to maintain the "public good". This utilitarian approach, which established the scope of Millian liberalism, described the political arena based on the conflict between the "personal interest" and the "collective interest" of the rulers. That made Mill the precursor of public choice theory. Unfortunately, Mill was never mentioned in the history and evolution of this theory.

According to Mill, no average ruler's behavior was completely or almost entirely determined by the ruler's perception of self-interest(s). The character and course of their actions were largely based on other causes (independent of any self-interest perception). The influence of current ideas that dominated the society, habitual emotions, general ideas, and actions were determined by the emotions, methods, and representative ideas of their social class. If these are neglected, we cannot understand how and based on what the ruler rules (Mill [1843] 1973, 891). "Sense of duty" and "philanthropy" were excluded since these traits already significantly govern the actions of almost every ruler. Here, Mill wanted to emphasize two significant factors that determine the character and course of ruler behavior: "self-interest" and "others". On the "others", the English philosopher wrote that when the influence of current ideas that dominate the society, habitual emotions, general ideas and actions is neglected, we cannot understand how and based on what the ruler rules (Mill [1843] 1973, 891).

To sum up, Mill identified two major categories that lead to the concept of the "principal interest of the rulers": the general factors that determine the decisions of the rulers (self-interest of the rulers, sense of duty, philanthropy) and other factors (the influence of current ideas in the society, habitual emotions, general ideas, and actions). In this categorization, the primary reasons that affected the behavior of the ruled corresponded to "general reasons", and the secondary reasons corresponded to "disturbance reasons".

The "disturbing factors/reasons" that constituted democracy, which Mill examined based on his philosophy of science, were the "national character" of each country determined by historical and cultural elements. These factors, to which the rulers are also subjected, affected the implementation of democracy. According to Mill, "national character" had a weight among the factors that affected the behavior of the people. That was the reason for the different approach to democracy in every country. Mill proposed a scientific branch he called "ethology" that aimed to investigate the factors behind that character because it was difficult to predict the "state of society" due to the unknown and unpredictable character of these factors. An American's behavior could seem strange to the French. According to Mill, national character should be specifically studied and described due to the nature and unpredictability of the events that it induced (Thierry 1994, 13).

In Millian and Tocquevillian philosophy, the significance of self-interest for rulers in government leads to problems in democratic functions. Their solutions were different for these problems, which was the fundamental difference of opinion between these two philosophers.

Mill argued that the election of well-educated and amenable rulers would be most beneficial for the people. He argued that this would allow the people to freely use their capacity for their self-interest, which would lead to an environment that could be governed with the least control. He claimed that this would be possible when elected rulers were true to the individual interests of the people, not only to their self-interest (Mill [1835 and 1840] 1977, 195–196).

Such a government approach was called "enlightened opinion" not "public opinion". Mill preferred the latter to the first. This was how Mill's elitist approach to politics began to shape. As Bouretz (1990) indicated, Mill began to advocate limited representation, based both on the American experience introduced by Tocqueville and on his readings on the uncertainties of the French Revolution. In doing so, he realized that he was beginning to resist democracy based on majority and defend the independence of the elites. For Mill, the best government was that of the "sage" (Bouretz 1990, 26).

The millennial "ruler elite" and the development of the US Constitution by economic elites were the embodiment of political capitalism. The economic and political order described by Mill was majoritarian pluralism, while what Schumpeter described was economic-elite domination (Beard 1913 cited by Holcombe 2015, 108). In the abovementioned case, the political elite acts as a "permanent bandit" (Olson 2000), both on their own and under the pressure of the economic elites, and manipulates the rules to maximize their interests.

This type of capitalism should also be interpreted based on minority and majority groups. The minority could allow the regulations and decisions that would transfer the resources of the majority to themselves. This, a function of majoritarian democracy, could also lead to the creative destruction described by Schumpeter. Here, neither democracy nor perfect competition exists.

## Government by the Elite: A Guarantee of Freedoms

A general look at the connection between democracy and capitalism, prominent in the Millian doctrine, would lead to such questions: Is the behavior of the ruling class elite leading to wealth or growth? The greater observance of which of the two abovementioned interests would lead to greater wealth or growth? What degree or type of democracy would lead to wealth or growth in the government of elites? The Millian approach to governance demonstrated that methodological individualism was the foundation of behavioral laws of not only the economic man (*homo economicus*) but also the political man.

The Millian government had two types: representative and despotic. Although the similarities (Akdere 2021) and inconsistencies between Mill's *Utilitarianism* and *On Liberty* have been analyzed, only a few studies were conducted on *The Representative Government*, where the theory of representative government was associated with the themes in these two books. Among these, E. Biagini investigated the influence of the Athenians on Mill's democratic ideas. N. Urbinati's book *Mill on Democracy* (2004) contributed significantly by developing the republican political theory (Tyler 2006).

The content and aim of the Millian theory of representative government were well described by Warner (2001). "Elites" and "elite citizens" were not the same thing. The latter sufficed to simply engage in politics and vote (Warner 2001). According to him, this theory was a "theory of articulated and responsible functional elites who represented different interests". Elites were categorized into three groups: (1) elite citizens, (2) wise representatives, and (3) skilled bureaucrats. He described the roles and responsibilities of each group, and relationships among them" (Warner 2001).

In the Millian framework, the role of elites in political analysis corresponded to the role of governors. According to Kurer (1989, 480), "it was argued that Mill introduced a coherent theory of government intervention that translated into straightforward policy proposals. The central task of the government was to foster progress: more justice and the improvement for men" (Kurer 1989, 480).

According to Mill, the government should be determined by the historical and institutional conditions in each country. In his words, the form of government was determined by "certain definite conditions". The free specification of this form was "amenable to selection". Based on the background developed by the Millian utilitarian philosophy, this reminds us of the idea that certain values could be violated for practical purposes. Mill did not say that there should be certain rules, values, or doctrines that determine government behavior. In contrast, he argued that the government can act with full creativity and ingenuity: "Forms of government are assimilated by any other expedients to attain human objects." (Mill [1861a] 1977, 37). The door was left wide open, and it was very clear that the duty of the government would be determined by the circumstances. He responded to this question quite clearly: "For, in the first place, the proper functions of a government are not fixed, but different in different states of society; much more extensive in a backwards state when compared to an advanced state" (Mill [1861a] 1977, 375). "For, government altogether being only a means, the eligibility of the means must depend on their adaptation to the end" (Mill [1861a] 1977, 383).

To what extent is the form of government by choice? Economist Mill responds to this question: "the trends for different forms of government to promote progress" (Mill [1861a] 1977, 378) and "totally an affair of invention and contrivance" (Mill ([1861a] 1977, 374). At this point, one suddenly realizes the danger: authoritarianism. However, before that point, a closer look at Mill's quest for the best form of government is warranted. How can we reach such a form of government? Mill's answer was step by step: "The first step is to define the purposes that should be promoted by the governments. The next is to inquire the best form of government that could reach these purposes" (Mill [1861a] 1977, 374).

The *Considerations on Representative Government* ([1861a] 1977) immediately demonstrates that it was written by a utilitarian philosopher. The book aimed to determine the function of a useful government. The first important clue was the employment of "expedient" instead of "useful" in line with utilitarian philosophy.

Mill's "government by the elite" revealed the differences between "personal interest" and "collective interest," as well as "utility" and "freedom". The outcome of the encounter between Millian political philosophy and moral philosophy was the prioritization of "personal freedoms" in every case; however, "personal freedoms" could be spoiled when they contribute to "personal interests". This approach to justice, called "loudable injustice", was the Millian method to resolve the conflict between moral and political issues. Only a government by the elite could acquire this reasoning and analytical skills. Freedoms could be neglected based on the decisions of such a government.

Who were the elites according to Mill? "They include individuals of proven qualities such as politicians, administrators and intellectuals, or, as Mill stated,' men of independent thought, who have by their writings or their exertions in some field of public utility, made themselves known and approved'" (Mill [1861a] 1977, 436–41, 456). He prioritized elites because "Mill assumed that it was only the elites who could properly assess the requirements of progress and the means to implement it" (Mill [1861a] 1977, 436–41, 448, 446–81). For Mill, "these were the individuals with the ability to secure progress, and, as Mill believed, most likely to be guided by ideas for the common good and not by narrow class interests. This requirement for the elite rule would imply a constitution that would assure ascendancy, it would have to involve substantial authoritarian elements" (Kurer 1989, 468).

The process that leads to authoritarianism was hidden in the answers given to the questions that asked for the 'best'. He responded to these questions with procedural individualism. For Mill, the development of the individual was the foundation of social development. Thus, there was a duality: both the rulers and the individuals in the society should have good qualifications (Barker 2015). Barker refers to Mil l: "If we ask ourselves what caused and conditioned good government in all senses, from the humblest to the most exalted, we would find that the principal, the one which transcended all others, was the qualities of human beings in the society over whom the government was exercised" (Mill [1861a] 1977, 388–389).

The current conflict between capitalism and democracy should be discussed based on the movements of interest groups, which are different from a social class (Holcombe 2015). The question of the best type of government, its functions, and its duties are based on the economic dimension. According to Baum (1999), the best government is the one that can intervene in different interests. For an expedient government, the form of government should be consistent with the people it aims to govern. Thus, the powers of society should be on its side. The form of this state, which should serve certain purposes, should be "expedient". This demonstrated that for Mill, practical objectives came before values. Government should serve practical purposes, and its aims and objectives should not be questioned: "government is conceived as a strictly practical art" (Mill [1861a] 1977, 374) and "raising no questions but only means and an end" (Mill [1861a] 1977, 374).

"Laudable injustice" leads to the intersection of democracy and capitalism. This could be explained with an example in Mill's book *The Subjection of Woman*, published in 1869. Although Mill was an advocate of women's liberation, he argued that married women should stay at home to take care of the home and men should work (Mill [1869] 1984). This idea, which was not akin to gender equality, restricted women's freedom. Its acceptability or appraisal depended on the improvement of the material wealth of the household by the division of labor between women and men. Mill's acceptance of this idea also indicated that he equated housework and wage labor (Gouverneur 2013).

Mill developed his idea about "majority rule" during the discussion of the boundary between 'personal utility' and 'collective utility.' Expression of concepts such as "majority rule" and public opinion demonstrated that Millian analysis pushed the limits of moral philosophy and opened the door for political philosophy. Mill, therefore, established a boundary between collective utility and individual utility. Admittedly, the individual should sometimes make sacrifices that would subsequently improve the collective happiness; however, since being virtuous and considerate improved public happiness, in Millian doctrine, these were associated with certain conditions where one can be called upon to consider the public utility; in all other cases, the private utility, interest, or happiness of a few people is all that needs attention.

However, individual interests should not always be sacrificed to improve public happiness, and individual liberties should also be protected from public interest. The contrast between individual and collective interest is the intersection between Millian moral and political philosophy. Mill discussed the Benthamite "majority rule" based on the boundary between "individual" and "collective" utilities. At the collective level, utility does not make sense for Mill because it could not be measured. Indeed, in Millian utilitarianism, "the greatest happiness" is immeasurable: according to Mill, social utility was not the sum of individual utilities. In other words, we could not reduce general utility to a simple sum of individual interests, the mechanical conception of happiness as defined by Bentham (Akdere 2021).

Some argued that Mill was not an advocate of democracy. Urbinati described his approach as "elitist republicanism". He implied that Mill tried to keep the majority out of politics, and this was "the role he ascribed to competent governance" (Tyler 2006, 351). Certain critics claimed that Millian liberalism presupposed restraint rather than the promotion of democracy. Mill proposed leaving certain issues to politically and intellectually 'mature' elites. According to Urbinati, "it was akin to the form of elitist republicanism that one finds in Machiavelli's Discourses on Livy, and its democratic features are tempered by (or realized through?) a Periclean belief that most of these features about the vote should be guided by deference to the views of their 'betters'" (Tyler 2006).

The danger for Benthamite utilitarianism is that when measuring the general interest, it allows the ignorance of personal interest as each interest fades away with the emphasis on behavior that only prioritizes general interest. Mill discussed this phenomenon based on a concrete description of the consequences: "Wherever all the forces of society act in one single direction, the just claims of the individual human being are in extreme peril. The power of the majority is salutary so far as it is used defensively, not offensively as its exertion is tempered by respect for the personality of the individual, and deference to superiority of cultivated intelligence" (Mill [1838] 1969, 108–9).

Democracy could become dangerous in its excesses (Warner 2001, 406). Aware of that fact, "Mill did not lead us toward democracy strictly, but toward a representative government with a heavy dose of skilled elites" (Warner 2001, 411). The warner called this structure "bureaucratic government", which is "a form of government in contrast with aristocracy, monarchy, or representative government" (2001, 411). Thus, "skilled bureaucrats" were a buffer to excessive democracy. Government should be limited to "legislation and administration". The government should not involve all members in these businesses but leave them to the elites called "skilled bureaucrats". According to Warner, Mill argued that the "essence and meaning of bureaucracy" was when "the government work is conducted by governors by profession". The government is described by Mill as "a specially trained group" and has "professional training, skill, and devotion". Their primary occupation is administration with the help of legislative commissions and the administrative body" (Warner 2001).

Here, elitism did not entail economic wealth but "special skills and experience in public administration". It was interesting that he annihilated "elected representatives" and strengthened the relations between "administrators and citizens" (Warner 2001). Mill expected not only skilled bureaucrats but also citizens: "Mill expected citizens with a qualified education, special public role, and superior occupational position to serve as opinion leaders who should be heard during public deliberation due to their special skills, knowledge, or experience" (Warner 2001). However, several theories articulated that citizens were not at all as conscious as Mill attributed. D. Williams (2021) introduced the concept of "rational" or "motivated ignorance" and "voter ignorance" in contemporary democracies and discussed ignorance and its costs in political life. For example, voting by ignoring the social damages of climate change. More specifically, "the costs of becoming informed massively outweigh the benefits of being informed" (Williams 2021, 7808).

However, if the economic dimension of these issues is not addressed, the examination of the relationship between collective benefit and personal benefit may be incomplete.

## The Economic Dimension of the Ideal State

Although Mill was among those who believed that there was a limit to growth (Zweig 1979; Maehara 2010), Mill tried to explain the reproduction of wealth, similar to Smith, Malthus, and Ricardo. He argued that even in a "steady state", this would be possible by preserving the capital stock, replacing the old with the new, and managing the unrenewable resources (Buckley 2011). According to Mill, the stationary state was "a necessary state in the progress of civilization" (Maehara 2010). In other words, the Millian ideal state was established on economic foundations. According to Schumpeter ([1954] 2006), the Millian "stationary state" was the state of a comfortable and economically developed society. G. Cleays (2019) shared this view and argued that wealth was not "boundless" for Mill. He argued that economic wealth would be replaced by a better quality of life in that state. Millian position was a stand against Ricardo. Ricardo considered the "stationary state" a "universal poverty without further progressive prosperity" (Cleays 2019).

Here, the mistake would be believing that Millian progress was limited to economics. As Kurer (1989, 5–6) argued, "at the heart of Millian concept of progress was the doctrine of the improvement of man towards more intellectual capacity and advanced moral standards". The most economical aspect in this statement was not that progress aimed individual freedoms but to change their "preferences" and "will". He explained what Mill meant with this idea of progress: "[t]his does not imply that Mill … wanted to force the adult populace to act against their will. He did, however, [seek to] create institutions that would change their will, either through an adequate structure of incentives, or by 'educating' them in particular political and economic institutions" (Kurer 1991 cited by McCabe 2021, 193).

Certain authors commented on Mill's discourse on the state's intervention in the economy and oligopolistic competition. Mill mentioned entrepreneurs and argued that they played a role in determining profits, differentiating their firms against competition (Rainelli 1983). R. F. Herber and A. N. Link (2006), citing Mill, claimed that the concept of the entrepreneur was introduced by Jeremy Bentham but developed by the Smith–Ricardo–Mill tradition. However, the term 'undertaker' employed by Mill did not reflect the full meaning. Mill described the 'undertaker' with capabilities such as "direction, control, and superintendence" (Mill [1848] 1965, 108) and argued that this individual had "superior business skills such as always producing a type of rent alongside ordinary profits" (Mill [1848] 1965, 476).

According to A. N. Link and J. R. Link (2009, 49), "Mill did not seriously entertain the idea of the entrepreneur as an innovator." For example, what he called "labor of invention and discovery" was nothing but wages. However, even more important was the theoretical approach that Herbert and Link (2006, 50) called the "unhappy alliance of the entrepreneur and the capitalist". In other words, the concept of "entrepreneur", the greatest virtue of which was creativity according to Schumpeter, was not present in the Millian narrative. Link and Link (2009) also claimed that Mill's *Principles of Political Economy* ([1848] 1965) contributed little to entrepreneurship theory. However, they argued that he expanded Cantillon's concept of "entrepreneur" and he considered the "entrepreneur" as "manager, gerent, or superintendent", similar to J.-B. Say (1767–1832), A. Marshall (1842–1924), and C. Menger (1840–1921).

T. W. Hutchison (1953 cited by Harris 1959, 604) compared Mill and H. Sidgwick based on their arguments on government intervention and stated that the former advocated nationalization through joint-stock corporations and oligopolistic industries. Citing Mill, he argued that every industry would eventually become oligopolistic, and the industries should eventually be nationalized. However, he also argued that this type of monopolization did not exist in Mill. Mill argued that joint stock companies would hardly survive if not in banking or insurance industries and added that "there were few instances of joint stock companies which were permanently successful without a monopoly" (Mill [1848] 1965, 139 cited by Harris 1959, 604). Hutchison noted that Mill discussed in Book II, chapter xv, paragraph 3 a concept called "practical monopolies". This type of monopoly exists in railways and related services, water and gas industries. However, Mill still did not mention privatization (nationalization) but argued that the water and gas industries should be managed by municipalities. According to him, "The railways might be owned but not operated by the state or owned and operated by private corporations subject to public regulation to assure reasonable prices" (Harris 1959).

P. Gillig and P. Légé (2017) focused on the reasons why Mill credited certain socialist projects in his analysis of the link and tension between liberalism and capitalism. Nevertheless, Mill opposed the idea that 'the economy will monopolize', advocated particularly by socialists. According to him, "the richest competitor neither does nor can get rid of all rivals, and exclusively possess the market, and it is not true that any important branch of industry or commerce formerly managed by many becomes, or shows a tendency to become, a monopoly of the few." Competition in an industry could be in the hands of two or three large companies at some point (Harris 1959, 608).

As argued by H. McCabe (2021), Millian socialism was unique. After the 1840s, under the influence of his discussions with Harriet Taylor, Mill started to see himself as a socialist; however, this socialism was not Marxist, Owenite, Fourierist, or Saint-Simonian. The issues of his socialism focused on local problems of cooperation rather than economic functions or type of government: "His form of socialism was decentralized, cooperative, and voluntarist. It was rooted in worker cooperatives, complemented by some state provision (preferably at the local level)" (McCabe 2021, 4).

G. Numa (2010) wrote that there were two types of monopolies in the Millian narrative: "practical monopoly" and "natural monopoly". However, Mill employed these two terms quite differently. In Book 2 Chapters 14, 15, and 16, he used "natural monopoly" to describe the plight of landowners and the rarity of skilled workers. According to Numa, he argued that the latter was the modern reflection of the former. Both concepts meant the same: "the benefits of a privileged or strategic position".

According to G. Mosca (1858–1941) (2008), natural monopoly was where "the subadditivity of cost functions (production costs less if it is manufactured by only one firm), and by sustainability (not-profitable entry)" or "natural monopoly was where there were barriers to entry in the market due to a technology characterized by economics of scale (i.e., declining average costs) in market demand". Mosca (2008) argued that classical economists described "natural monopoly" but not quite well. According to Mill, these were not an outcome of a law but a spontaneous monopoly (Mill [1848] 1965 cited by Mosca 2008, 323). This spontaneous monopoly was either due to "entry barriers induced by capital requirements or a consequence of combinations" or technology dependence. Sharkey (1982, 14; Hazlett 1985: 2 cited by Mosca, 2008; Numa, 2010) argued that the first economist who introduced the idea of technology-dependent monopoly was Mill, and Walras also employed the same term when he mentioned transportation networks such as railways, roads, and canals.

Mill's ideas on monopoly also included the definition of the elites. The entrance to the market, where this spontaneous monopoly existed, was only open for those with high capital to make a profit. Thus, he argued that trade in this market would be controlled by a few players. Postal services, gas and water companies ([1848] 1965) were his examples. "Large scale was preferable in small-scale production", because, for technical reasons associated with economics of scale, it was better to have a company that satisfy the entire market than to have several companies that satisfy only a piece of the market (Sharkey, 1982; Mosca, 2008).

This share grows so much over time that the state also wants to have a piece of it as competition decreases: "When … a business of real public importance can only be carried on advantageously upon so large a scale as to render … competition … illusory … it is much better to treat it at once as a public function" (Mill [1848] 1965, 142 cited by Mosca, 2008). Mill puts that this is where "competitors are so few, they always agree not to compete" (Mill [1848] 1965, 142 cited by Mosca, 2008). The process that allows the highest profit for all in the market, whether through government intervention or minimal competition, is also a dynamic the leads to the development of elites.

What kind of policy maker would Mill be? Or how would Mill apply this theory to practical politics? Would he tolerate the interference of the state in the national economy? We could only speculate about the answers. According to Kurer (1989), "Mill formulated two rules that were candidates for a theory of government intervention. The first rule was based on the distinction between the actions based on self and the other, where government intervention would be restricted to actions of the second kind" and "the second rule was the principle of laissez-faire, where nonintervention was the general rule." (Kurer 1989).

We still have not answered Skorupski's (2006) question "Why read Mill today?" According to him, both liberals and non-liberals described Millian liberalism as "powerful" and "comprehensive". However, the former were glad that Mill introduced the moral dimension, and the latter were glad that he introduced the enemy. We, on the other hand, argued that Mill should be read today since it provides the most useful political environment for modern democracy by incorporating both moral and economic dimensions. Today, we could argue that democracy would be quite incomplete without the economic dimension. The economic dimension is located at the "blind spots" that Mill left as he analyzed the relationship between democracy and capitalism. These "blind spots" could be resolved by considering the "disturbing causes" while the "general causes" are applied. Skorupski (2006, 106) argued that, "Millian liberalism functioned as a political practice" and introduced the idea that Millian philosophy proposed a "practice" beyond an ethical vision or philosophy.

## References

Akdere, Ç. 2021. *L'Arrière-plan philosophique de l'économie politique de John Stuart Mill.* Paris: Classiques Garnier.

Audard, C. 1998. Présentation. In *L'Utilitarisme Essai sur Bentham*, ed. J.S. Mill, 3–18. Paris: PUF.

Ball, T. 2000. The Formation of the Character: Mill's 'Ethology' Reconsidered. *Polity* 33 (1): 25–48.

Barker, Chris. 2015. Mass and Elite Politics in Mill's Considerations on Representative Government. *History of European Ideas* 41 (8): 1143–1163.

Baum, B. 1999. J. S. Mill's Conception of Economic Freedom. *History of Political Thought* 20 (3): 494–530.

Beard, C. 1913. *An Economic Interpretation of the Constitution of the United States*. New York: Macmillan.

Bentham, J. 1785–6. Principles of the Civil Code. In *The Works of Jeremy Bentham*, ed. J. Bentham, 189–266. Part. VII. Edinbourg: Tait.

———. [1789] 1970. *An Introduction to the Principles of Morals and Legislation*. London: University of London The Athlone Press.

Bilir, H., and M. Şahin. 2021. Politik Ekonomiye Schumpeterci Bir Bakış: Kapitalizm Ve Siyasi Elitler. *Pamukkale Üniversitesi Sosyal Bilimler Enstitüsü Dergisi* 43: 263–276.

Boudon, R. 1985. L'individualisme méthodologique. *In Encyclopedia Universalis* 2 (Supplément): 644–647.

Bouretz, P. 1990. Préface. *Sur la liberté* J. S. Mill [1859] 1990, 13–60. Paris: Éd. Gallimard.

Buckley, M. 2011. John Stuart Mill and the Idea of a Stationary State Economy. In *Humanistic Ethics in the Age of Globality*, ed. Claus Dierksmeier, 137–147. London: Palgrave Macmillan.

Cleays, G. 2019. *Mill and the Stationary State*. Kyoto Conference 2019 on James Mill and John Stuart Mill / Classical Political Economy, September 11–12.

Cot, A.L. 1992. Jeremy Bentham, un 'Newton de la morale'. In *Nouvelle Histoire de la Pensée Economique: Des scolastiques aux classiques*, ed. A. Béraud and G. Faccarello, vol. 1, 289–304. Paris: La Découverte.

Cuche, D. 2004. *La notion de culture dans les sciences sociales*. Paris: La découverte.

Cunningham, F. 2002. *Theories of Democracy: A Critical Introduction*. London: Routledge.

Fagot-Largeault, A. 2002. L'ordre Vivant. In *Philosophie des sciences*, ed. D. Andler and A. Fagot-Largeault, vol. 2 Vols, 483–572. Paris: Éd. Gallimard.

Gillig, P., and P. Légé. 2017. De La Défiance à L'éloge Des Coopératives Par J. S. Mill: Retour Sur La Constitution D'une Pensée Libérale Dans La Première Moitié Du Xixe Siècle. *Cahiers d'économie Politique* 73 (2): 197–221.

Gouverneur, V. 2013. Mill versus Jevons on traditional sexual division of labour: Is gender equality efficient. *The European Journal of the History of Economic Thought* 20 (5): 741–775.

Green, E. J. 2019. J. S. Mill's Liberal Principle and Unanimity. *Papers* 1903.07769, arXiv.org.

Halevy, E. 1901–1904. *La formation du radicalisme philosophique*. Paris: Alcan.

Harris, Abram L. 1959. J. S. Mill on Monopoly and Socialism: A Note. *Journal of Political Economy* 67 (6): 604–611.

Hazlett, T. 1985. The Curious Evolution of Natural Monopoly Theory. In *Unnatural Monopolies: The Case for Deregulation Public Utilities*, ed. R.W. Poole, 1–25. Lexington, MA: Lexington Books.

Herbert, R.F., and A.N. Link. 2006. Historical Perspectives on the Entrepreneur. *Foundations and Trends R in Entrepreneurship* 2 (4): 261–408.

Holcombe, Randall G. 2015. Politik Kapitalizm (Political Capitalism). Translated by Atilla Yayla. *Cato Journal* 35 (1): 103–125.

Hutchison, T.W. 1953. *A Review of Economic Doctrines. 1870–1929.* Oxford: Oxford University Press.

Kahan, A. S. 1992. *Aristocratic Liberalism. The Social and Political Thought of Jacob Burckhardt, John Stuart Mill, and Alexis de Tocqueville.* Oxford: Oxford University Press.

Kurer, O. 1989. John Stuart Mill on Government Intervention. *History of Political Thought* 10 (3): 457–480.

Leary, D.E. 1982. The Fate and Influence of John Stuart Mill's Proposed Science of Ethology. *Journal of the History of Ideas* 43 (1): 153–162.

Lewes, G.H. 1879. *The Problems of Life and Mind.* London: Trübner & Co.

Link, A. N., and J. R. Link. 2009. *Government as Entrepreneur.* Oxford: Oxford University Press.

Maehara, N. 2010. John Stuart Mill's Theory of the Stationary State in Connection with the Law of the Falling Rate of Profit. *Political Economy Quarterly* 47 (3): 79–90.

Marshall, A. [1890] 1920. *Principles of Economics.* London: Macmillan and Co. (E-Book by Liberty Fund, Inc.)

McCabe, H. 2021. *John Stuart Mill Socialist.* Montréal: McGill-Queen's University Press.

Mill, J. [1824] 1992. *Education. Supplement of the Encyclopaedia Britanica.* In *James Mill Political Writings.* Cambridge: Cambridge University Press.

———. [1835] 1977. De Tocqueville on Democracy in America I. In *Essays on Politics and Society*, ed. J. M. Robson, and A. Brady, 47–61, Collected Works. vol. XVIII. Toronto: Toronto University Press.

———. [1836a] 2003. On the Definition of Political Economy; and on the Method of Investigation Proper to It. In *Essays on Economics and Society*, ed. L. Robbins, and J. M. Robson, 309–340. Collected Works. Vol. IV. Toronto: Toronto University Press.

———. [1836b] 1977. State of Society in America. In *Essays on Politics and Society*, ed. J. M. Robson, and A. Brady, 91–117, Collected Works. Vol. XVIII. Toronto: Toronto University Press.

———. [1838] 1969. On Bentham. In *Essays on Ethics, Religion, and Society*, ed. J. M. Robson, F. E. L. Priestly, and D. P. Dryer, 75–117, Collected Works. Vol. X. Toronto: Toronto University Press.

———. [1840] 1977. *De Tocqueville on Democracy in America II.* In *Essays on Politics and Society*, ed. J. M. Robson, and A. Brady, 153–205, Collected Works. Vol. XVIII. Toronto: Toronto University Press.

———. [1843] 1973. *A system of logic ratiocinactive and Inductive*, ed. F. E. L. Priestly and J. M. Robson, Collected Works. Vol. VII–VIII. Toronto: Toronto University Press.

———. [1848] 1965. *Principles of Political Economy.* Collected Works. Vol. II–III. Toronto: Toronto University Press.

———. [1859] 1977. On Liberty. In *Essays on Politics and Society*, ed. J. M. Robson, and A. Brady, 213–310, Collected Works. Vol. XVIII. Toronto: Toronto University Press.

———. [1861a] 1977. Considerations on Representative Government. In *Essays on Politics and Society*, ed. J. M. Robson, and A. Brady, 371–579, Collected Works. Vol. XIX. Toronto: Toronto University Press.

———. [1861b] 1969. Utilitarianism. In *Essays on Ethics, Religion, and Society*, ed. J. M. Robson, F. E. L. Priestly, and D. P. Dryer, 203–261, Collected Works. Vol. X. Toronto: Toronto University Press.

———. [1869] 1984. Subjection of Women. In *Essays on Equality, Law and Education*. ed. J. M. Robson and S. Collini, 259–341, Collected Works. Vol. XXI. Toronto: Toronto University Press.

———. [1873] 1981. *Autobiography*. In *Autobiography and Literary Essays*, ed. J. M. Robson and J. Stillinger, 60–229, Collected Works. Vol. I. Toronto: Toronto University Press.

———. [1873] 1993. *Autobiographie*. Translated into French by G. Villeneuve. Paris: Aubier.

Mitchell, Wesley C. 1918. Bentham's Felicific Calculus. *Political Science Quarterly* 33 (2): 161–183.

Mosca, M. 2008. On the Origins of the Concept of Natural Monopoly: Economies of Scale and Competition. *The European Journal of the History of Economic Thought* 15 (2): 317–353.

Mouchot, C. 2003. *Méthodologie Economique*. Paris: Éd. du Seuil.

Nikolić, D. 2015. Practopoiesis: Or How Life Fosters a Mind. *Journal of Theoretical Biology* 373: 40–61.

Numa, G. 2010. Note sur le monopole naturel et le monopole pratique chez J. S. Mill. *Revue économique* 61 (2): 341–352.

Olson, M. 2000. *Power and Prosperity: Outgrowing Communist and Capitalist Dictatorships*. Oxford: Oxford University Press.

Persky, J. 2016. *The Political Economy of Progress John Stuart Mill and Modern Radicalism*. Oxford: Oxford University Press.

Rainelli, M. 1983. Entrepreneur et profits dans les "Principes" de John Stuart Mill et d'Alfred Marshall. *Revue économique* 34 (4): 794–810.

Robson, J. M. 1989. Introduction. In *Autobiographie*. J. S. Mill. [1873] 1993. Paris: Aubier.

Roquet, L. 1889. Introduction. In *Les Principes d'Economie Politique*, J. S. Mill. [1848] 1889, I–LI, Paris: Guillaumin.

Rousseau, J.-J. [1750] 2002. *The Social Contract and The First and Second Discourses*, ed. Susan Dunn. New Haven and London: Yale University Press.

Schumpeter, J. A. [1954] 2006. *History of Economic Analysis*. London: Routledge Taylor & Francis eLibrary.

Sharkey, W.W. 1982. *The Theory of Natural Monopoly*. Cambridge: Cambridge University Press.

Sigot, N. 1995. *L'utilitarisme benthamien à la rencontre de l'économie classique*. PhD Thesis defended in Université Paris I Panthéon-Sorbonne. Paris: France.

———. 2001. *Bentham et l'économie, Une histoire d'utilité*. Paris: Economica.

Skorupski, J. 2006. *Why Read Mill Today?* London: Routledge.

Smart, P. 1992. Mill and Nationalism. National Character, Social Progress and the Spirit of Achievement. *History of European Ideas* 15 (4-6): 527–534.

Thierry, P. 1994. Présentation. In *Essais sur Tocqueville et la société américaine*. J. S. Mill. [1835] 1994. Translated by P.-L. Autin et al. Paris: Vrin.

———. 1998. Présentation. In *L'utilitarisme. Essai sur Bentham*. J. S. Mill. [1835] 1994. Translated into French by C. Audard and P. Thierry, 147–161. Paris: PUF.

Thilly, F. 1923. The Individualism of John Stuart Mill. *The Philosophical Review* 32 (1): 1–17.

Thompson, Dennis F. 1976. *John Stuart Mill and Representative Government*. Princeton, NJ: Princeton University Press.

Touchard, J. [1958] 1985. *Histoire des idées politiques*, Vol. 2. Paris: PUF.

Tyler, C. 2006. Review Article: Elitism and Anti-elitism in Nineteenth Century Democratic Thought. *History of European Ideas* 32 (3): 345–355.

Urbinati, N. 2002. *Mill on Democracy. From the Athenian Polis to Representative Government*. Chicago and London: University of Chicago Press.

———. 2006. *Representative Democracy: Principles and Genealogy*. Chicago: University of Chicago Press.

Varouxakis, G. 2002. *Mill on Nationality*. London and New York: Routledge.

Ward, L. 2022. Chapter 6. John Stuart Mill and the Stationary State. In *Recovering Classical Liberal Political Economy: Natural Rights and the Harmony of Interests*, 151–179. Edinburgh: Edinburgh University Press.

Warner, Beth E. 2001. John Stuart Mill's Theory of Bureaucracy within Representative Government: Balancing Competence and Participation. *Public Administration Review* 61 (4): 403–413.

Williams, D. 2021. Motivated Ignorance, Rationality, and Democratic Politics. *Synthese* 198: 7807–7827.

Wilson, F. 1990. *Psychological Analysis and the Philosophy of John Stuart Mill*. Toronto: University of Toronto Press.

Xiao, Y. 2021. John Stuart Mill on China's Stationary State. *History of Political Economy* 53 (5): 833–856.

Zouboulakis, M.S. 2005. On the Social Nature of Rationality in Adam Smith and John Stuart Mill. *Cahiers d'économie Politique* 49: 51–63.

Zweig, K. 1979. Smith Malthus Ricardo and Mill: The forerunners of Limits to Growth. *Futures* 11 (6): 510–523.

CHAPTER 4

# Schumpeter on Capitalist Development, Creative Destruction and Elites

**Abstract** The intellectual interest in Schumpeter increased significantly after J. A. Schumpeter's (1883–1950) concepts, such as innovation, creative destruction, and entrepreneurship, were employed to explain the rapid economic changes in the 1980s. As Schumpeter proposed, innovations accelerated capitalist development rapidly while leading to serious economic instability. Schumpeter argued that the success of capitalism, not failure, would lead to instability. While innovations rapidly dismantle the old economic structure, they give way to a new one. Furthermore, since computer technology was based on data-intensive technologies in the 1990s, only large companies could adapt to rapid developments. Therefore, innovations and competition increased the monopolistic tendencies in the economy, leading to a growth company size. The fact that markets rely on monopolistic competition rather than free competition would inevitably lead to the power of interest groups and control of the government by the elites.

**Keywords** Capitalist development • Creative destruction • Elites • Representative democracy



G. Baş Dinar, Ç. Akdere, *Tensions Between Capitalism and Democracy Today From the Perspective of J. S. Mill and J. A. Schumpeter*, https://doi.org/10.1007/978-3-031-45547-6_4

During rapid technological advances induced by the internet and computer technologies after the 1990s, Schumpeter became a significant economist due to his approach to innovation, entrepreneurship, and creative destruction. These concepts were employed to explain the rapid advances and changes in the economy in the 1990s based on J. A. Schumpeter's (1883–1950) analysis of capitalism in *Capitalism, Socialism and Democracy*[1] ([1942] 2008). The rapid economic developments induced by technological advances prioritized the evolutions and changes emphasized by Schumpeter. Nelson and Winter's "*An Evolutionary Theory of Economic Change*" published in 1982 led to the revival of the evolutionary economics school, the roots of which go back to Veblen. In that book, the authors' emphasis on Schumpeter's ideas and their frequent references to Schumpeter led to the recognition of the latter as the founder of the evolutionary school of economics (De Liso 2022, 141).

> The influence of Joseph Schumpeter is so pervasive in our work that it needs a special emphasis. Indeed, the term "neo-Schumpeterian" would be adequate to describe our entire approach as evolutionists. (Nelson and Winter 1982, 39)

The intellectual interest in Schumpeter increased significantly after Schumpeter's concepts, such as innovation, creative destruction, and entrepreneurship, were employed to explain the rapid economic changes in the 1980s (Juma 2014; Hagedoorn 1996). The most important economist who explained the change in Western capitalism with these concepts was Schumpeter. The analysis that Schumpeter based on creative destruction was popular during the 1990s (Diamond 2006; DeLong and Summers 2001; Rosenberg 2000).

Schumpeter's concepts of innovation, entrepreneurship, and creative destruction were quite successful in explaining the rapid technological advances in the 1990s (Kleinknecht 1990). As Schumpeter proposed, innovations accelerated capitalist development rapidly while leading to serious economic instability. Schumpeter argued that the success of capitalism, not failure, would lead to instability. Innovations rapidly dismantle the old economic structure, giving way to a new one (Reinert and Reinert 2003, 56). Furthermore, since computer technology was based on

[1] Hereafter *CSD*.

data-intensive technologies in the 1990s, only large companies could adapt to rapid developments. Therefore, innovations and competition increased the monopolistic tendencies in the economy, leading to a growth company size. As Schumpeter proposed, the perfect competition model, on which the classical economy was based, was not profitable. Not to fail in capitalist competition, firms had to grow (Schumpeter [1942] 2008, 104, 105).

The fact that markets rely on monopolistic competition rather than free competition would inevitably lead to the power of interest groups and control of the government by the elites. According to Schumpeter, the driving force behind entrepreneurial capitalist development is competition. Entrepreneurs differ from other individuals based on several characteristics. The entrepreneur is an elite due to his or her qualifications and functions in capitalism. Throughout the book, Schumpeter spoke highly of individuals with these superior qualities and believed that an entrepreneur with these superior qualities who supervises social and economic development should have a privileged position in society.

Schumpeter's analysis of democracy entailed an analogy of the economy and the entrepreneur. He also applied classical free competition to democratic operations and the parliamentary system. Similar to economic competition that ensures an effective distribution of economic resources, a similar law of competition should be enacted in politics. However, before this analysis, Schumpeter criticized classical democracy theory. Based on this criticism, he argued that the only possible form of democracy was representative democracy, reducing politics to elections.

There was a significant correlation between Schumpeter's analyses of capitalism and democracy (Elliott 1994, 281). His ideas in *CSD* indicated these parallels. Schumpeter's analysis of the elite was generally separated from his analysis of capitalism. Schumpeter was considered one of the most important democratic elite theoreticians. However, these theories were insufficient since they distanced Schumpeter's ideas on elites from the context of political economy, in other words, from his analysis of capitalism. Thus, Schumpeter's views on elites and democracy require a holistic approach to the analysis of capitalism.

Schumpeter's analysis of the elites could help understand the economic policies of today. In modern capitalism, elites or interest groups play key roles in capitalist functions and the control of the state apparatus. Today, the increasing role of elites cannot be understood only with political analysis. As Schumpeter stated, the increased power of elites was a result of the long evolution of the capitalist system.

Schumpeter strongly emphasized that capitalism was an evolutionary system in *CSD*. In this book, Schumpeter emphasized that capitalism was a dynamic and developing system and argued that capitalism would fall victim to its own success and inevitably collapse at the end. Thus, he agreed with Marxist predictions that capitalism could not be sustained and was doomed to collapse as a logical consequence of its functioning. However, unlike K. Marx (1818–1883), he did not assign a transformative role to labor class in social change; thus, he did not adopt the idea that capitalism would be terminated by a revolution. According to Schumpeter, the failure of the system would not be the end of the capitalist system, as Marx suggested. In contrast, its own success would be the end of capitalism. It would rot the social institutions over time and inevitably prepare the conditions for its self-destruction (Schumpeter [1942] 2008, 81–86).

In *CSD*, Schumpeter initially argued that capitalism was a dynamic and open system and then included an economic analysis that revealed internal instability of this system due to the concept he coined creative destruction, which leads to capitalist development but also a monopolistic system. Schumpeter's analysis in *CSD* was an analysis of instability. Schumpeter emphasized that capitalism was inherently prone to instability (Schumpeter 1928). The monopolistic tendency of capitalism, which would inevitably lead to its collapse, was based on this analysis of instability. Thus, Schumpeter's ideas on democracy should be analyzed based on his analysis of capitalism.

First and foremost, Schumpeter analyzed capitalism based on an evolutionary approach (Shionoya 2007; Fagerberg 2003; Andersen 1994). He first attempted to determine the dynamic nature of capitalism and the basic motivation behind capitalist development. However, Schumpeter never thought that capitalism would grow and survive indefinitely. In contrast, he agreed with Marx that profit rates would inevitably decrease during capitalist development, which in turn would reduce the willingness of entrepreneurs to invest. Since the capitalist system is based on profits and entrepreneurs invest as long as they make a profit, the system would become increasingly unstable and endanger its own existence. However, unlike Marx, Schumpeter emphasized that capitalism would collapse due to its success, not failure. This analysis of instability, which he based on creative destruction, was the foundation of Schumpeterian theory. The disappearance of the entrepreneurial spirit and the increasing creativity in capitalism, the loss of innovation, bureaucratization, and a series of social institutional changes would end capitalism. Schumpeter argued that capitalism was not a sustainable system and wrote a comprehensive economic and political analysis of its causes and consequences.

The connection between Schumpeterian economic and political analysis was induced by his methodology. Schumpeter described science as "any conscious effort to improve knowledge" in *the history of economic analysis.* In the same work, he emphasized that science could be defined as "special techniques developed to understand and interpret reality in any field of knowledge", underlining the technical aspect of science, and described science from a sociological perspective as "a field that combines certain scientific research, scientists, or researchers". Thus, he argued that a set of techniques were available for the scientific economist, unlike other individuals who think, talk and write about economic issues. He stated that economists employ techniques such as economic theory, economic history, statistics, and economic sociology in economic analysis (Schumpeter [1954] 2006, 10).

These definitions demonstrated Schumpeter's broad approach to science. Since each of these fields is complementary, Schumpeter indicated that the collaboration between these fields was extremely important in economic analysis. In his article "*The Creative Response in Economic History*" (1947), he emphasized the benefits of the collaboration between economic theorists and historians (Schumpeter [1947] 1991, 221). Furthermore, Schumpeter described the daily behavior and philosophy of individuals with pre-analytical vision and emphasized that pre-analytical vision had a great impact on science by influencing the value judgments and attitudes of scientists.

His methodology allowed Schumpeter to broaden his economic approach. Thus, he avoided a purely economic analysis and analyzed economic events based on political, sociological, and historical factors. This approach allowed Schumpeter to establish a correlation between economic and political, social and historical categories. In contrast with the abstract analysis of neoclassical economists, he provided a holistic analysis that focused on psychological, historical, sociological, and economic factors (Baş Dinar 2022, 145, 146).

Schumpeter's interest in evolution and change was the main reason for his methodology and theoretical analysis. However, this should not mean that Schumpeter considered the abstract theoretical analysis of neoclassical economics futile. In contrast, Schumpeter was particularly impressed by

L. Walras's (1834–1910) concept of equilibrium in his early academic life and believed that equilibrium analysis could allow the comprehension of the transformation of the economy from a state of equilibrium to a state of disequilibrium. However, Schumpeter considered static analysis useful in understanding disequilibrium, and the analysis of disequilibrium and instability was the main objective of Schumpeter's economic analysis (Güler Aydın 2011, 192–200).

## Schumpeterian Analysis of Capitalism

The Schumpeterian approach to economics was holistic and accounted for the technical and theoretical aspects of economics, as well as institutional and historical phenomena that shaped human behavior. The most important work where he employed this methodology was *CSD*, published in 1942. In this work, he emphasized that capitalism was a dynamic and advancing system and analyzed the factors behind capitalist development. Due to his holistic methodology, Schumpeter was concerned with not only the economic but also the political, social, and institutional consequences of capitalist development. Thus, Schumpeter argued that capitalist development led to social progress and economic development. Arguing that certain social rights that shaped modern civilization emerged with capitalist initiative, Schumpeter emphasized that capitalist development led to both social and economic progress in *CSD* (Schumpeter [1942] 2008, 69).

Schumpeter emphasized the success and individual entrepreneurship in capitalist society and argued that the capitalist system was more successful than other systems due to the desire of the entrepreneur to profit and resulting innovations (Schumpeter [1942] 2008, 73). In a capitalist society, entrepreneurs should make the right decisions to lead in a competition and to survive. According to Schumpeter, this competition was not only an economic struggle. The pressure of competition threatened the entrepreneurs with bankruptcy or change of class. Income determines the social position of both individuals and families in a capitalist society. Thus, Schumpeter underlined the fact that individuals should be in a constant struggle for success not only to rise in their class but also to remain in their class (Schumpeter [1942] 2008, 73, 74). Schumpeter emphasized that the success of the entrepreneur determined not only economic but also social existence. The competitive pressures not only affected the entrepreneur economically but also led to an anxiety about losing social status. Thus, Schumpeter focused on both social and economic factors in his analysis.

According to Schumpeter, the main difference between capitalist and previous societies was rational reasoning. Schumpeter argued that rational reasoning developed a scientific approach and led to innovations that paved the way for capitalist development. Additionally, rational reasoning weakened the old aristocratic feudal classes due to meritocracy and allowed individuals to rise with success and improve their social status. According to Schumpeter, the possibility of rising in meritocratic capitalist society was the main difference between capitalist and pre-capitalist societies. In pre-capitalist societies, strict hierarchical classes prevented transition from one class to another, in other words, social progress. However, capitalist society allowed individuals to improve their income, and their improved economic reputation allowed social progress. Schumpeter emphasized that rational reasoning was not limited to economic organizations and led to the organization of all aspects of social life (Schumpeter [1942] 2008, 124, 125). Schumpeter indicated that rational reasoning was behind capitalist development and was interested in the effects of rationalization on social life, not just economic life.

Schumpeter emphasized that scientific knowledge that emerged due to rational reasoning led to innovations, which in turn led to rapid economic and social changes in capitalism. According to Schumpeter, no external factors such as wars, revolutions and population growth were behind the rapid developments in capitalism. Although these factors created the conditions for capitalist development, they were not the causes of capitalist development. According to Schumpeter, the main factor that activated capitalism was innovation. Schumpeter described these innovations as the development of new consumer goods, new modes of production, discovery of new markets, and foundation of new industrial organizations (Schumpeter [1942] 2008, 82, 83). According to Schumpeter, these innovations led to constant change and the emergence of new modes that constantly destroyed the old in capitalism. Schumpeter called this creative destruction the main factor behind capitalist development. Not to fail in competition, all capitalists eventually had to keep up with this development. It was not possible for capitalists who could adapt to change to survive (Schumpeter [1942] 2008, 83).

In a system where competition plays such a key role, every entrepreneur resorts to protective measures such as keeping the means of production a secret and signing long-term agreements to preserve investments. On the other hand, industries closely follow the activities of rival firms to avoid falling behind in competition. More entrepreneurial and more competitive businesses innovate more. These competitive and innovative firms need to increase total production by adopting new means of production and maintaining their investments in the market. Entrepreneurs should closely follow new means of production or businesses that develop novel products or industries to have a realistic idea about business strategies. The main characteristic of these innovative enterprises is entrepreneurship and high competition. These competitive and innovative firms aim to increase total production and gain competitive advantages over other firms in the market via new means of production (Schumpeter [1942] 2008, 88, 89).

Schumpeterian analysis demonstrated that competition was a dominant force in capitalism. According to Schumpeter, capitalist competition led to innovations and capitalist development while promoting the collapse of the capitalist system. Schumpeter employed the concept of creative destruction to emphasize this duality in competition. Because it led to capitalist development and innovations, the entrepreneur is the driving force and the most important actor of the system (Mc Caffrey 2009, 6). Schumpeter described the function of entrepreneurs as "is to reform or revolutionize the pattern of production by exploiting an invention or, more generally, an untried technological possibility for producing a new commodity or producing an old one in a new way, by opening up a new source of supply of materials or a new outlet for products, by reorganizing an industry and so on" (Schumpeter [1942] 2008, 132). Thus, the entrepreneur could develop a new product based on new technical advances, a new mode of production for an old commodity, discover a new raw material, or reorganize an industry. These innovative activities have significant effects on the economy and welfare. Schumpeter based his economic analysis on the entrepreneur and innovations. However, the development of these innovations, which could have a significant impact on the economy, was not easy. Because these innovations are inconsistent with the usual economic requirements, society can often reject them. Furthermore, to innovate, entrepreneurs should possess certain capacity, knowledge, and skills. Additionally, the discovery or invention of new commodities and modes of production are not sufficient for entrepreneurship. Entrepreneurs need to implement these discoveries or inventions and profit from them (Schumpeter [1942] 2008, 132).

According to Schumpeter, the entrepreneur could be the driving force of capitalist development and innovate only under monopolistic capitalism. Thus, in a perfect competition market that includes several buyers and sellers, none of which could affect the price and modes of production, new commodities, or new modes of production could not be easily developed due to the small size of these companies. Schumpeter emphasized that it would be quite difficult for small firms to adopt new modes of production, and a perfect competition market, the theoretical foundation of neoclassical economics, could not serve capitalist development. Since monopolistic capitalism that includes giant enterprises was the only way to increase total production in the long term, Schumpeter indicated that maintenance of perfect competition was wrong for the state via the regulation of certain industrial activities (Schumpeter [1942] 2008, 106). According to Schumpeter, the entrepreneur could no longer be the driving force of economic development, and individual entrepreneurship would be replaced by the bureaucracy, obstructing capitalist development. Additionally, the rise of monopolistic capitalism would end in the collapse of the sociopolitical value system and capitalist society (Schumpeter [1942] 2008, 134–139).

Schumpeter indicated that capitalist development would inevitably strengthen the opposition to capitalism, and the bourgeoisie could only defend its interests with rational and nonviolent means due to rationalization in capitalist society. Thus, Schumpeter argued that the bourgeoisie could only employ economic pressures on the people, weakening their political power. According to Schumpeter, the bourgeoisie is aware of its weak political power and abstains from involvement in political issues. This leads to a bourgeoisie unprepared for potential national and international problems. Schumpeter emphasized that due to its political weakness, the bourgeoisie required a protective net that included non-bourgeois elements such as the aristocracy. However, Schumpeter also emphasized that this protective class disappeared after the development of the capitalist system. According to Schumpeter, the weakening of this protective layer was another reason for the interruption of capitalist development (Schumpeter [1942] 2008, 137, 138).

According to Schumpeter, although innovations and capitalist development were only possible in monopolistic capitalism, the latter was also an obstacle to capitalist development in the long run. In monopolistic capitalism, production and innovation are conducted by professional R&D departments in large corporations, not by individual entrepreneurs.

Schumpeter described this as follows: "progress itself may be mechanized as well as the management of a stationary economy, and this mechanization of progress may affect entrepreneurship and capitalist society" (Schumpeter [1942] 2008, 131–134). This situation may prevent capitalist development by weakening the entrepreneurial spirit.

The only negative outcome of the advanced rationalization induced by capitalist development was not the weakening of the entrepreneurial spirit. Schumpeter argued that rationalization would gradually spread to private life and lead to radical changes in bourgeois families. The increase in rationalization would create individuals who prioritize costs and profits, leading to a dramatic change in the traditional gender roles in the family. The size of the family would shrink since child-rearing would increasingly be considered burdensome and birth control would be prevalent. Additionally, the spread of rational reasoning transforms interpersonal relations. Over time, this would lead to the rejection of traditional gender roles. Furthermore, rationalization would lead to individual psychological transformations; the desire to enjoy life would lead to new expenses such as travel and entertainment. Thus, fundamental changes would be observed in family values and individual lifestyles (Schumpeter [1942] 2008, 157–160).

As mentioned above, Schumpeter argued that capitalism would inevitably evolve into monopolistic capitalism. Innovations, which are of vital importance for capitalist development, were only possible in monopolistic capitalism. However, Schumpeter claimed that the emergence of large corporations in monopolistic capitalism would destroy the freedom of ownership and contracts, which are the basis of capitalist institutions. The evolution of capitalism toward monopoly would change the nature and control of ownership in previously private corporations. With the growth of company size, these would no longer be managed by the families but by professional executives. Thus, the controlling power of the capital owners would be significantly reduced, and corporate decisions would be made by bureaucrats who own limited shares in the company. Professional executives would be either ineffective or inadequate in important issues such as increasing profitability and productivity, or they would manage the company based on self-interest rather than corporate interests (Schumpeter [1942] 2008, 141, 142), leading to a decrease in the entrepreneurial spirit and developmental dynamics of capitalism.

Schumpeter indicated that in addition to these negative effects of the changes in the ownership structure in monopolistic capitalism, freedom of contract would be seriously damaged as well. According to Schumpeter, in monopolistic capitalism, contracts would gradually become anonymous and bureaucratic, no longer individualistic. Additionally, corporate shareholders do not contribute to future financial, political, and physical corporate decisions (Schumpeter [1942] 2008, 142). Schumpeter interpreted this as the exclusion of the right to property and argued that capitalist development would harm its essence.

Thus, the factors that could lead to the collapse of capitalism in Schumpeterian analysis were not purely economic. Schumpeter explained the collapse of capitalism with a series of psychological, sociological, cultural, and political factors. Schumpeter argued that the disintegration of capitalism would be from within (Schumpeter [1942] 2008, 161, 162). Schumpeter described these developments, which included social, psychological, legal, and economic factors, as "the opposition of capitalist development to its own social order". In this analysis, Schumpeter revealed that capitalist development harmed the factors that were the reason for the existence of the capitalist class.

According to Schumpeter, capitalist development would increase welfare and create an opposition of workers and intellectuals against the capitalist system, capitalists, and entrepreneurs. Schumpeter explained the opposition to capitalism with a social individual he coined "the intellectual". Schumpeter indicated that intellectuals were not a uniform social class like peasants or workers. Schumpeter argued that the opposition of intellectuals to capitalism would increase gradually. Schumpeter believed that the capitalist system tended to self-destruct, which was observed as a slowdown of development in the initial stages and would eventually lead to the collapse of capitalism. Schumpeter argued that the factors that would hinder the development of capitalism and pave the way for its collapse would not only destroy capitalism but lead to a socialist civilization.

In short, Schumpeterian theory based the success of the capitalist system on the success and skills of the individual entrepreneur. Entrepreneurs produced economic innovations due to their critical mind, intuition and comprehension skills, will, and leadership. Although the historical use of critical reasoning led to the replacement of the superior functions of the entrepreneur by ordinary executives and the fall of capitalism by its success, Schumpeter idealized the traits of the entrepreneur. Rationalization, entrepreneurship, and creative destruction not only accelerated capitalist development but also led to the collapse of capitalism. However, certain developments in capitalism would interrupt the competition based on entrepreneurs and innovations and harm capitalist economic development. This does not mean that capitalism would suddenly disappear. Capitalist modes of production would be sustained under monopolistic capitalism; however, individual entrepreneurs and innovation would cease to be the engine of economic development, and thus, the basic developmental impulse of capitalism would be weakened. This would gradually lead to the complete disappearance of the capitalist system and prepare the conditions for socialism (Baş Dinar 2022, 147, 148).

Schumpeter clearly discussed his views on democracy and elites in *CSD* (1942). Similar to other elite theorists, Schumpeter began his analysis with a criticism of the Marxist analysis of social classes. Thus, before moving on to Schumpeter's analysis of the elite, his objections to Marxist class theory should be discussed. Schumpeter indicated that Marxist separation of social classes was not systematic, although this was one of the main points of his theory. According to Schumpeter, a rough categorization of social classes based on the ownership of the means of production was insufficient (Schumpeter [1942] 2008, 14).

Furthermore, Schumpeter emphasized the fact that Marxist claims that class struggle would destroy the capitalist system signified the problem of primitive accumulation. According to Schumpeter, the question of the original capital of the capitalists was one of the most significant issues in Marxist analysis. Schumpeter opposed Marx's claim that the idea that certain individuals were capitalists due to their superior intelligence, capacity or savings was a "myth" and emphasized that this approach was the truth to a certain extent, although it may look like a myth at first glance. Thus, Schumpeter opposed the idea that people were the members of the classes they were born into, indicating that intelligence, skills and individual achievements were extremely important. Individuals could climb to higher social classes based on their individual efforts, talents, and intelligence. This was a fundamental contradiction with Marxism. Schumpeter claimed that excessive intelligence and energy would significantly determine industrial success (Schumpeter [1942] 2008, 16).

Thus, Schumpeter believed that individual effort, talent, and intelligence played a key role in capital accumulation and emphasized the fact that these elements lead to circulation across class boundaries. According to Schumpeter, Marxist class analysis significantly ignored human effort. There was an important correlation between Marxist class theory and the economic interpretation of history. According to Marx, the first theory conditioned the second and limited its scope, assigned a special meaning to it, and determined the means and conditions of production. Production means establishing the social structure, and social structure determines all aspects of civilization, political history, and culture (Schumpeter [1942] 2008, 18, 19).

The analysis in Schumpeter's *CSD* included two parts. The first part argued that the capitalist system was the victim of its success and prone to collapse. Thus, Schumpeter initially analyzed the dynamics of this process, which he called "creative destruction". Although Schumpeter's analysis emphasized the role of social and cultural changes, it was essentially an economic analysis (Requejo 1991). Second, Schumpeter proposed a theory of democracy based on competition, similar to economic theory. In this section, Schumpeter's theory of democracy and his ideas about the role of elites in the democratic process are addressed based on his analyses included in *CSD*.

## Criticism of the Classical Democracy Theory

Schumpeter described democracy in the eighteenth century as "the institutional arrangement for arriving at political decisions which realizes the common good by making the people itself decide issues through the election of individuals who are to assemble in order to carry out its will" (Schumpeter [1942] 2008, 250). Schumpeter criticized classical democracy theory based on this description. Thus, he first objected to "the common good and will of the people". This discourse asserted that every member of the society would participate in the efforts to fight the bad by asserting the good based on a common goal, understanding their responsibilities. It was suggested that all members of the society collectively controlled public affairs. Schumpeter significantly objected to this idea by stating that there was no such thing as a certain common good accepted by the whole public or that could be accepted due to a rational consensus because certain people could desire things different from the common good. Additionally, the predetermined common good could be different for different individuals and social groups. Furthermore, even when it is assumed that an adequate level of common good exists for all, it cannot solve certain problems. For example, although everyone wants to be healthy, some may not want to comply with public health requirements such as vaccination. Additionally, ideas about the predefined common good could constantly change. Thus, Schumpeter argued that the basis of the classical democracy that people act based on the common good was not accurate (Schumpeter [1942] 2008, 251, 252).

Schumpeter also denied the concept of the will of the people in the description of classical democracy. According to Schumpeter, to talk about the will of the people, everyone should know their exact demands from the government. Additionally, to talk about the presence of such a will, each individual could observe the events, interpret them accurately, and critically filter the available data, rather than adopting random acts and slogans. However, according to Schumpeter, essentially personal political decisions cannot be considered the will of the people, even when the ideas and desires of each citizen are perfectly known, and everyone acts with ideal speed and rationality based on this knowledge. This would lead to inconsistency between the political decisions and what the people truly want (Schumpeter [1942] 2008, 253, 254).

Schumpeter based his objection on the idea of a will determined by human personality and acts on the multidimensional property of human behavior. Schumpeter emphasized the rational and irrational aspects of human behavior. Additionally, human behavior could change with social pressures. He exemplified the sudden disappearance of moral restraints, civilized ideas, and emotions and the sudden emergence of primitive reflexes and infantile behavior during excitement, emphasizing that the human nature on which the classical democracy was based was unfounded. Underlining that the same assumptions were also valid in economics, Schumpeter criticized the dominant economic approaches. He underlined the fact that consumer demand and preferences were not predetermined, rational, and rapid, as argued by these theories. He emphasized that consumers were affected by commercials in real life and that they could not control production, as suggested by the prevailing economic approaches. In contrast, constant advertising affects consumer decisions (Schumpeter [1942] 2008, 256–257).

Thus, Schumpeter proposed an analogy between individuals' political decisions and economic decisions. Both the dominant economic philosophy and the classical democracy theory claimed that human behavior was defined by political and economic processes. Schumpeter emphasized that this assessment was inadequate and unrealistic in several respects. Both analyses considered human behavior to be extremely mechanical, predetermined, and predictable. On the other hand, Schumpeter emphasized that human intentions and actions were more complex and talked about the relative certainty of desire and rationality of behavior (Schumpeter [1942] 2008, 258).

In this framework, Schumpeter emphasized that voters had individual ideas, dreams, and desires independent of society. The voter preserved individual views and attitudes and employed these subjective views in political decisions. Schumpeter also underlined that there was no activity (other than voting) where an ordinary citizen could reflect personal will on national issues. Schumpeter characterized the private citizen as "he is a member of unworkable committee, the committee of the whole nation, and this is why he expends less disciplined effort on mastering a political problem than he expends on a game of bridge" (Schumpeter [1942] 2008, 261).

Schumpeter also indicated that as soon as the typical citizen is in the political arena, the mental achievements of that citizen are reduced. Because individuals discuss and analyze political decisions based on their real interests, they are easily influenced by others. Thus, the typical citizen conforms to irrational prejudices and reflexes in political issues, which could also reduce moral standards (Schumpeter [1942] 2008, 261–263). Although Schumpeter claimed that the will of the people was impossible, he also claimed that politics form a will of the society, an artificial will that could be described as the will of the people, albeit quite broadly. Thus, according to Schumpeter, the will of the people was an artificial product of politics, which does not reflect the real will of the people (Schumpeter [1942] 2008, 262).

Schumpeter attributed the reason the classical doctrine of democracy was still in currency despite these shortcomings and misconceptions about humans and society and the lack of empirical evidence to dogmatic ideological attitudes. The defense of these principles by the followers of classical democracy was dogmatic, almost like a religion. Furthermore, since the classical doctrine of democracy was based on historical events and developments in several nations, the approach has been easily accepted by these nations. The principles proposed by the advocates of classical democracy have been strongly supported in these countries since democratic revolution led to freedom and independence. However, the differences between these principles and the practice became evident over time. Furthermore, there are societies where the principles of classical doctrine have been implemented successfully. For example, the democratic doctrine could be successfully implemented in small and primitive societies or in countries such as Switzerland without significant problems in public policy. Finally, the preference for this rhetoric by politicians flattened the masses and became an excellent tool not only to evade responsibility but also to crush the opposition in the name of the people, allowing the classical approach to democracy to survive despite its shortcomings (Schumpeter [1942] 2008, 264–268).

## From Economic Competition to Political Competition

Schumpeter defined democracy based on the criticism of the classical democracy discussed in the previous section. Thus, "the democratic method is that institutional arrangement for arriving at political decisions in which individuals acquire the power to decide by means of a competitive struggle for the people's vote" (Schumpeter [1942] 2008, 269). Schumpeter argued that this description could eliminate the shortcomings of classical theory. Schumpeter's description emphasized the significance of leadership in democracy. However, classical theory ignored the role of leadership by assigning an arbitrary role to the electorate in democracy. For example, politicians who include certain political demands in election campaigns and those who support these demands play a key role in the fulfillment of these demands, such as unemployment insurance (Schumpeter [1942] 2008, 270).

In his definition, Schumpeter emphasized the role of leadership and described democracy mainly based on the concept of "competition for leadership". Thus, Schumpeter underlined the similarity between political and economic competition, establishing another analogy between economics and politics. Schumpeter later rephrased "leadership competition" as "to free competition for a free vote" (Schumpeter [1942] 2008, 271). According to Schumpeter, the most legitimate democratic method of competition was elections. However, there could always be unfair or fraudulent competition methods such as leadership via military insurrection. Thus, perfect competition was not possible in political life as in economic life. As it is not always possible to ensure free competition in the economic market, political competition in democracy could lead to certain practical problems. In other words, the competition among political leaders could be unfair or imperfect, similar to the economy (Schumpeter [1942] 2008, 271).

Schumpeter's description of democracy as a competition for leadership allowed the clarification of the relationship between democracy and individual freedoms. Schumpeter emphasized that democracy did not necessarily guarantee greater personal freedom when compared to other regimes under the same conditions. However, when democracy is described as a competition for leadership, the association between individual freedoms and democracy can be easily established. In democracies, political leaders should have the freedom, at least in principle, to present themselves to the electorate and compete for political leadership, which requires considerable freedom of discussion. This, in turn, required freedom of the press. For a functional democracy and for leaders to fulfill their representative duties, the political climate should allow individual freedoms. Democracy can only function in an environment of individual freedoms. However, Schumpeter emphasized that the relationship between democracy and individual freedoms was not always strong. In certain cases, this relationship could be weakened or interrupted by various factors. On the other hand, Schumpeter emphasized that the idea that voters not only elect but also control the government should be approached with caution. Thus, Schumpeter underlined the fact that after electing the government, the elector had no control other than not re-electing the government in the next election (Schumpeter [1942] 2008, 271, 272).

Based on the abovementioned ideas, it could be suggested that there was a correlation between the economic and political analysis of Schumpeter. According to him, individuals could achieve important economic and political positions, not as members of a class but as individuals. Thus, there is competition between individuals in both politics and economics. As highly competitive entrepreneurs introduce new production techniques and create new commodities, competitive politicians play a more significant role in political decisions. Thus, Schumpeter's concept of competition was the basis of both his political and economic analyses.

## Democracy as a Function of Competition and Elites

Schumpeter discussed how his democracy theory would work in practice. The primary function of the electoral vote in a democracy was to form a government, in other words, to elect the council of ministers. In the national government, the government was practically meant to decide on the head of government (leader). Schumpeter emphasized that the political leadership of the prime minister included three separate elements and led to the power of each prime minister. Thus, the prime minister was primarily elected as the head of the party. As soon as the prime minister takes office, he also becomes head of the parliament. Thus, the prime minister could influence other parties and their members. Finally, under normal conditions, the prime minister leads the constituency in the party organization. According to Schumpeter, the prime minister creatively determines and executes the ideas of the party. The prime minister eventually rises beyond party politics toward a constructive leader of public opinion. This gives significant powers to the leader (Schumpeter [1942] 2008, 274, 275).

According to Schumpeter, in the parliamentary system, forming the government is the duty of the parliament. Parliament normally decides who would be the prime minister, but the parliament is not entirely free to do so. The hands of the MPs are tied not only by party politics but also by the individual they selected (Schumpeter [1942] 2008, 277).

Schumpeter described the cabinet as a joint product of the parliament and the prime minister. The prime minister proposes cabinet member appointments. Parliament could both accept and affect these appointments. From the party's point of view, the cabinet is a subordinate collection of leaders, reflecting the party. From the prime minister's point of view, the cabinet is not just a group of war allies but a small parliament that includes party members who defend their self-interests and views. The cabinet plays a specific role in terms of the prime minister, party, parliament, and voters in the democratic process. This intermediary leadership function is associated with daily work performed by individual cabinet members in various departments. According to Schumpeter, this function was not associated with fulfilling the will of the people in every case (Schumpeter [1942] 2008, 278).

According to Schumpeter, parliament has several other tasks besides forming a government. First, the parliament is a legislator; furthermore, it has several administrative functions, such as the budget. The foremost and primary aim of every political party is to defeat the other parties to form or sustain the government. Schumpeter indicated that political decisions such as conquest or war are the raw material, not the aim, of parliamentary activities. Thus, parliamentary decisions on national issues mainly aim at the sustenance or disposal of the government. In other words, parliamentary decisions either approve or disapprove the leadership of the prime minister. Thus, each vote is a vote of confidence that determines the power of the leader (Schumpeter [1942] 2008, 278–280).

Although Schumpeter emphasized the power of the leader in the political system, he also argued that no leadership was absolute. Democratic leadership was less absolute when compared to others due to competition, which was the essence of democracy. In this approach, theoretically, every individual under the leader's command had the right to take the place of the leader. Thus, the governed had a choice between unconditional submission to the leader's standards or setting self-standards. The leader also had two choices: discipline or ambiguous authority. Thus, groups, supporters, or individual members could voice their legislative proposals (Schumpeter [1942] 2008, 280, 281).

The selection of the electorate often determines the outcome of elections. This is part of the democratic process. Voters do not make decisions about outcomes and issues. Voters do not elect the members of parliament from a broad-minded group of eligible individuals. According to Schumpeter, under normal conditions, the candidate who makes a move for the parliamentary seat has the upper hand. Voters accept or reject this move by comparing it with that of other candidates (Schumpeter [1942] 2008, 282).

Schumpeter objected to the classical definition of the party as a group of individuals who aim to promote public welfare. According to Schumpeter, this definition was dangerous. This definition of the political party would lead to the assignment of certain principles by the parties. These principles would determine the success of that party for its members. Schumpeter indicated that principles could not define a party. According to Schumpeter, a party is a group whose members agree to act jointly in a competitive political arena for power. Thus, the party functions based on competition, similar to a corporation. Tools such as ads, slogans, and marches employed by the party administration were not only accessories. According to Schumpeter, these were the foundation of politics (Schumpeter [1942] 2008, 283).

In short, Schumpeter opposed the classical approach to democracy that described democracy as the rule of the people. Democracy, according to Schumpeter, was a system where the people could accept or reject the rulers. In a democracy, future leaders compete for the votes of the electorate. Once the ministers are appointed, they constantly compete with their opponents, although they cannot be demoted easily by the parliament. The prime minister should watch for his opponents at all times and constantly lead his supporters, intervene in any conflict and the measures under discussion, and control his cabinet. The failure or defeat of a government is often associated with the physical exhaustion of the prime minister or government leaders. In other words, there is constant competition to secure or to maintain power. As a result of this competition, the government should first consider the political value of a political position, a bill, or an administrative act. It is extremely difficult for politicians to serve the long-term interests of the nation since the abovementioned facts impose a short-term perspective on authority. Schumpeter indicated that foreign policy was often ignored for the sake of domestic policies (Schumpeter [1942] 2008, 286, 287), invalidating the argument that democracy represents the interests of the people the best. Leaders who do not wish to lose the competition prefer the political decisions that would keep them in power or bring them back to power, but not those that would serve the social interests the best.

After he described the democratic method and discussed democratic functions, Schumpeter emphasized that there were four conditions for the success of democracy. These conditions merged Schumpeter's with the Millian elitist approach. First, the politician should have superior qualifications. Elected party members and cabinet members should possess the qualifications to fulfill their responsibilities. According to Schumpeter, for such politicians, a political social class, a product of a strict selection process, should be created. This class should be neither too closed nor too easily accessible by outsiders. Schumpeter emphasized that the creation of such a class, in addition to introducing individuals who were successful in other political fields, would ensure the establishment of a professional order.

Thus, the professionalism of the political class would be improved (Schumpeter [1942] 2008, 290, 291). According to Schumpeter, another necessary condition for the success of democracy was the proximity of the sphere of influence of political decisions (Schumpeter [1942] 2008, 291, 292). The third was the availability of a well-trained bureaucracy with a strong sense of duty and unity, good training and tradition in public affairs adequate for a democratic government in modern industrial society (Schumpeter [1942] 2008, 293). The bureaucracy should not only be efficient in administration but also be strong enough to guide and train political leaders when necessary. Thus, it should develop its own principles and have the independence to implement them (Schumpeter [1942] 2008, 293).

Here, Schumpeter re-emphasized the significance of the human element. Similar to the case of political class, the issue of available human material (qualified human capital, as mentioned by Mill and Schumpeter) was crucial in politics. Furthermore, for such a class of bureaucrats to fulfill their duties, there should be a social class. According to Schumpeter, this class should be neither too rich nor too poor. It should also have neither very ordinary nor very different traits. Schumpeter argued that these conditions would lead to "democratic self-control" (Schumpeter ([1942] 2008), 294). Schumpeter believed that these conditions would lead to parliaments and constituencies with high moral and mental properties to withstand the proposals of deceitful and eccentric individuals. According to Schumpeter, parliament members should resist the temptation to overthrow or agitate the government whenever they can. If they do, successful policies cannot be implemented. Those who support the government should accept the leadership role, let the government be limited by a program and let it run. Additionally, they should consent to the leadership of a shadow cabinet by the opposition and, within certain limits, allow them to conduct political activities and even political struggle (Schumpeter [1942] 2008, 293).

According to Schumpeter, resisting this would be the beginning of the end of democracy. Voters outside the parliament should respect the division of labor between them and the elected. They should not lose their confidence easily between the elections, and after they elect someone, they should understand that political activity was the business of the elected, not theirs. Furthermore, to ensure effective competition in leadership, a wide tolerance should be present for differences of opinion (Schumpeter [1942] 2008, 295, 296).

Schumpeter discussed the relationship between capitalism and democracy after he criticized the classical democracy doctrine and described his version of democracy. He emphasized that modern democracy was a product of capitalism; therefore, there was causality between democracy and capitalism (Schumpeter [1942] 2008, 297). He initially developed a democracy model of political competition based on free competition in the economy. However, Schumpeterian capitalism theory proposed that capitalist development would hinder competition and would gradually evolve into a monopolistic economy. For competition in economy and politics, state influence on the economy should be limited. Thus, the relationship between liberalism and democracy was only possible with a minimal state. The bourgeois would limit the political sphere based on the ideal of the minimal state and limited public authority.

According to Schumpeter, the minimal state was extremely important to legalize the bourgeoisie and allow autonomous individual effort.

However, Schumpeter emphasized the absence of such a minimal state under twentieth century capitalism. Therefore, Schumpeter underlined that bourgeois democracy was valid under quite specific historical conditions. These historical conditions no longer existed under monopolistic capitalism in the twentieth century during his lifetime. Thus, the minimal state, which was the mainstay of classical democracy, had no practical application. In contrast, Schumpeter mentioned that the sphere of public activity would expand with the evolution of capitalism into a monopolism. The expansion of the public sphere of activity could threaten democracy by reducing individual freedoms.

However, Schumpeter did not deduce that there would be no democracy in the bourgeois economic order. Although he indicated the decline in democracy, he emphasized that when democracy was strong, it provided equal opportunities for both individuals and families and it also improved personal freedoms. According to Schumpeter, a capitalist society was well qualified for democracy. In a society founded on individual interest, it was easier to limit individuals when compared to societies dominated by the state. The bourgeoisie, which pursued private interests, tended to tolerate political differences and respected radical ideas as long as they were not against their interests. However, Schumpeter argued that when these conflicted with the interests of the bourgeoisie, the latter could easily neglect democratic principles. Thus, according to Schumpeter, certain deviations from democracy could be observed with organized capitalist interests. Then, the means of special interests they possessed could be used to thwart the general will of the people. These special tools could be used to interfere with the Schumpeterian competitive leadership mechanism (Schumpeter [1942] 2008, 296–298).

## References

Andersen, E.S. 1994. *Evolutionary Economics: Post-Schumpeterian Contributions.* USA: Pinter.

Baş Dinar, G. 2022. Schumpeter'in kapitalizm analizi üzerine yöntemsel ve teorik bir değerlendirme. *Ömer Halisdemir Üniversitesi İktisadi ve İdari Bilimler Fakültesi Dergisi* 15 (1): 129–148.

De Liso, N. 2022. Joseph Alois Schumpeter. In *A Brief History of Economic Thought from the Mercantilists to the Post-Keynesians*, ed. H. Bougrine and L.P. Rochon. Cheltenham: Edward Elgar.

DeLong, J. B., and L. H. Summers. 2001. The 'New Economy': Background, Questions and Speculations. *Federal Reserve Bank of Kansas City Economic Review* (Fourth Quarter): 29–59.

Diamond, A.M., Jr. 2006. Schumpeter's Creative Destruction: A Review of the Evidence. *The Journal of Private Enterprise* 22 (1): 120–146.

Elliott, J.E. 1994. Joseph A. Schumpeter and The Theory of Democracy. *Review of Social Economy* 52 (4): 280–300.

Fagerberg, J. 2003. Schumpeter and the Revival of Evolutionary Economics: An Appraisal of the Literature. *Journal of Evolutionary Economics* 13: 125–159.

Güler Aydın, D. 2011. Schumpeter'de denge, dengesizlik ikilemi: Walrasçı ve Marxçı vizyonlar. In *İktisadı Felsefeyle Düşünmek*, ed. O. İşler and F. Yılmaz, 189–204. İstanbul: İletişim Yayınları.

Hagedoorn, J. 1996. Innovation and Entrepreneurship: Schumpeter Revisited. *Industrial and Corporate Change* 5 (3): 883–896.

Juma, C. 2014. Complexity, Innovation, and Development: Schumpeter Revisited. *Policy and Complex Systems* 1 (1): 1–21.

Kleinknecht, A. 1990. Are There Schumpeterian Waves of Innovations? *Cambridge Journal of Economics* 14 (1): 81–92.

Mc Caffrey, M. 2009. Entrepreneurship, Economic Evolution, and the End of Capitalism: Reconsidering Schumpeter's Thesis. *The Quarterly Journal of Austrian Economics* 12 (4): 3–12.

Nelson, R.R., and S.G. Winter. 1982. *An Evolutionary Theory of Economic Change*. London: Belknap Press of Harvard University Press.

Reinert, H., and E. S. Reinert. 2003. Creative Destruction in Economics: Nietzsche, Sombart, Schumpeter. *The Other Canon Foundation Working Paper*. http://www.othercanon.org/papers.

Requejo, F. 1991. Elitist Democracy Or Liberal Democracy? Schumpeter Revisited. *Working Paper* 42. https://core.ac.uk/download/pdf/13283385.pdf.

Rosenberg, Nathan. 2000. *Schumpeter and the Endogeneity of Technology: Some American Perspectives*. London: Routledge.

Schumpeter, J.A. 1928. The Instability of Capitalism. *The Economic Journal* 38 (151): 361–386.

———. [1947] 1991. The Creative Response in Economic History. In *Essays*, ed. R.V. Clemence, 221–231. USA and UK: Transaction Publishers.

———. [1954] 2006. *History of Economic Analysis*. Great Britain: Taylor and Francis eLibrary.

———. [1942] 2008. *Capitalism, Socialism and Democracy*. New York: First Harper Perennial Thought Edition.

Shionoya, Y. 2007. Schumpeter and Evolution: A Philosophical Interpretation. *History of Economic Ideas* 15 (1): 65–80.

CHAPTER 5

# Conclusion: How Mill and Schumpeter Tell Us Today?

**Abstract** The review of the ideas of J. S. Mill (1806–1873) and J. A. Schumpeter (1883–1950) on democracy, political participation and elites has demonstrated that these were complementary in many points. Mill criticized J. Bentham (1748–18832) for assigning too much weight to the decisions of the majority. Similarly, Schumpeter opposed the concept of the "common good and will of the people". Second, both philosophers, although they are prominent defenders of methodological individualism, widened their limits by treating human nature in the social sphere and the complexity of the human mind. Third, as Millian approached democracy as a state of society, Schumpeter discussed democracy based on the competition for leadership. Fourth, according to Mill, the interests of the rulers were based on the fear of maintaining or losing power. Similarly, Schumpeter emphasized that the primary goal of every political party was to defeat others to come to power or stay in power. Fifth, both emphasized that the rulers should be well educated and highly qualified for democracy to function. Finally, both Mill and Schumpeter criticized the classical approach that described democracy as the rule of the people or the will of the people.

**Keywords** Democracy • Capitalism • Methodological individualism • J. S. Mill • J. A. Schumpeter • Elite



G. Baş Dinar, Ç. Akdere, *Tensions Between Capitalism and Democracy Today From the Perspective of J. S. Mill and J. A. Schumpeter*, https://doi.org/10.1007/978-3-031-45547-6_5

There are important similarities between the analyses of both thinkers in terms of the relationship between democracy and capitalism, the limitations of the understanding of participatory democracy, and their emphasis on the role of elites in political and economic processes. In this book, it is argued that J. S. Mill (1806–1873) can contribute to the understanding of twenty-first century capitalism in many ways through his observations of nineteenth-century capitalism, and J. A. Schumpeter (1883–1950) is the one who has the best description of it. Today, elites dominate decision-making processes to an increasingly critical extent rather than a pluralistic democratic understanding. The fact that elites are increasingly effective in directing economic and political processes has brought them to the focus of economic and political research.

The dynamics of capitalism today are not different from those experienced in the nineteenth century. Issues such as capital accumulation and distribution, the scale of production, and the centralization of capital are still current. Those associated with democracy are mostly multidimensional and related to capital accumulation and distribution. These dimensions led to the diversification of the concept of capital, that is, the accumulation of capital through encroachment, expansion privatization, control of multinational corporations and state policies. Thus, Mill and Schumpeter approached economic and political aspects holistically in their discussion of capitalism. To understand the current conflict between capitalism and democracy, the conflicts experienced in the Millian era in the nineteenth century and the Schumpeterian one in the twentieth century are discussed.

The review of the ideas of Mill and Schumpeter on democracy, political participation and elites demonstrated that these were complementary. It was observed that Schumpeter, a twentieth century philosopher, prioritized representative democracy and political participation and the role of elites in politics established by Mill in the nineteenth century. This complementarity can be summarized by describing the similarities and differences between them. It is possible to summarize this similarity in a few points.

First, both objected to the classical approach to democracy, which was described as the rule of the people. Mill criticized J. Bentham (1748–18832) for assigning too much weight to the decisions of the majority. Similarly, Schumpeter opposed the concept of the "common good and will of the people". Like Mill, he criticized the classical notion that all members of society jointly conduct public affairs in democracy. Initially, he emphasized that there was no such thing as the common good that would be accepted by all or be compelled to accept due to its rationality because common good constantly changes. Similarly, he emphasized that there was no such thing as the will of the people. For such a will to emerge, the individual should be rational, and everyone's desires should be both predetermined and rational. Even then, according to Schumpeter, it was impossible to consider the resulting decisions as the will of the people. Decisions made by such a will could be different from what people truly want.

Second, both philosophers, although they are prominent defenders of methodological individualism, widened their limits by treating human nature in the social sphere and the complexity of the human mind. This approach was the baseline for the representative democracy approach. Thus, Mill criticized Benthamite and Hobbesian's *a priori* description of cases and human tendencies and *a priori* foundation of political inferences (Thierry 1998, 157). Inspired by the Alexis De Tocqueville (1805–1859), Tocquevillian method that employed deduction and induction, Mill believed that empirical inferences played a key role in the exploration of the laws of the human mind. Thus, Mill argued that the decisions and behaviors of rulers could only be understood by spatial, temporal, and environmental analysis. Therefore, the Millian approach was quite similar to that of Schumpeter who argued that human nature could not be simplified and it entailed a complex mechanism.

The Millian corpus would suggest that his approach to capitalism was based on the social and political history of the system. Schumpeter offered an alternative to Marx by criticizing his description of human history as the history of class conflict. He divided society not into classes but into culturally homogeneous groups with distinct cultural identities and social solidarity. According to him, the economic status of individuals could not classify individuals as in Marxism, but the differences between individual aptitudes that assign different functions to these groups in society. In fact, this approach was quite nationalist. Mill allowed for the development of individual skills via education as the foundation of both social and economic progress. The individual who was open and susceptible to the development of all types of skills via education was the foundation of the society for him.

Schumpeter, like Mill, emphasized that human behavior was multifaceted. By underlying the relationship between the individual's political and economic decision-making processes, Schumpeter criticized both classical economic and classical democratic theories' analysis of political and economic developments that shaped human behavior. Both economists argued that political or economic processes could not be explained by such a reductionist approach to human nature. Additionally, both generalized these findings to all social sciences, including economics and political science. Schumpeter emphasized that human intentions and actions were quite complex and spoke about the relative certainty of desires and rationality of behavior. This approach would make it impossible for a collective will, which could also be described as the will of the people, to emerge. Thus, the possible democracy according to Schumpeter, similar to Mill, was a different type of representative democracy. Both Mill and Schumpeter advocated that economic progress in different societies was induced by different elite groups. For example, the Schumpeterian definition of democracy considered it a "practice". Thus, democracy did not mean government by the people but only the election of elites who would govern them (Bilir and Şahin 2021). This applies to the Millian government of the elites or political elites.

Third, as the Millian approach considered democracy as a state of society, Schumpeter discussed democracy based on the competition for leadership. Due to his adoption of the philosophy of science, Mill emphasized the complexity of the causes that comprise the state of society. Thus, based on his premise, several factors, such as social classes and interclass relations, tastes, character and aesthetic development, and wealth and its distribution, should be considered to comprehend the state of society. Differences between these factors that prevail in different countries lead to differences between democracies in these countries. A similar multidimensional analysis could be found in Schumpeter. In *Capitalism, Socialism and Democracy* [1942] 2008, he discussed different societies and historical processes and emphasized, like Mill, that democratic practices differed both between societies and historical periods.

Fourth, Mill first tried to explain how people could look after their interests in a democratic order. As such, he emphasized that the factor that determined the interests of the rulers was generally their self-interest. According to Mill, the interests of the rulers were based on the fear of maintaining or losing power. Similarly, Schumpeter emphasized that the primary goal of every political party was to defeat others to come to power or stay in power. Thus, according to Schumpeter, parliamentary decisions on national issues were mainly based on the maintenance or neglect of power. Unlike Mill, Schumpeter explained the efforts to preserve power with the competition between leaders. Thus, each vote means a vote of confidence and determines the power of the leader against her or his opponents. Furthermore, both Mill and Schumpeter argued that the actions of the rulers were generally determined by self-interest; however, they emphasized that there were other reasons as well. Elements such as the influence of contemporary ideas that dominate society, emotions, ideas, etc., of their social class worked in the background. If these are neglected, it would not be possible to understand how the rulers ruled.

Fifth, both discussed the conditions required for an effective democracy. Both emphasized that the rulers should be well educated and highly qualified for democracy to function. Mill argued this based on the concept of "enlightened opinion". As a result, he defended the "rule of the wise", while Schumpeter emphasized that politics should be a profession, and an elite stratum should be educated as human resources for politics. The existence of such a stratum would ensure both the political engagement of people with various experiences and the development of certain professional standards for politics. Thus, this would improve the qualifications of potential politicians who aspire to power.

Finally, Schumpeter and Mill emphasized that the development of individual rights and liberties was necessary for a functional democracy and for leaders to fulfill their representative duties. Thus, both Mill and Schumpeter criticized the classical approach that described democracy as the rule of the people or the will of the people. Both advocated a different type of representative democracy in contrast to the majority rule, where elites played a key role in that representative democracy. Both indicated that it was important to ensure the independence of the elites. The review of Mill and Schumpeter's ideas on democracy, political participation and elites reveal that these were consistent. Schumpeter, a twentieth century philosopher, prioritized the representative democracy and political participation approach developed by Mill in the nineteenth century and his ideas about the role of elites in democracy.

## References

Bilir, H., and M. Şahin. 2021. Politik Ekonomiye Schumpeterci Bir Bakış: Kapitalizm ve Siyasi Elitler. *Pamukkale Üniversitesi Sosyal Bilimler Enstitüsü Dergisi* 43: 263–276.

Schumpeter, J.A. [1942] 2008. *Capitalism, Socialism and Democracy.* New York: First Harper Perennial Thought Edition.

Thierry, P. 1998. Présentation. In *L'utilitarisme. Essai sur Bentham.* J. S. Mill. [1835] 1994. Translated into French by C. Audard and P. Thierry, 147–161. Paris: PUF.

# Index





G. Baş Dinar, Ç. Akdere, *Tensions Between Capitalism and Democracy Today From the Perspective of J. S. Mill and J. A. Schumpeter*, https://doi.org/10.1007/978-3-031-45547-6

Printed in the United States
by Baker & Taylor Publisher Services